Schiffy

The Life and Times of Somebody
You Probably Don't Know, But Should

David "Schiffy" Schiff

With Steve Penn

www.TotalPublishingAndMedia.com

ISBN: 978-1-63302-239-3 (Paperback)
ISBN: 978-1-63302-257-7 (Hardcover)
ISBN: 978-1-63302-260-7 (E-Book)

TABLE OF CONTENTS

DEDICATION

This book is for all the friends, family, colleagues and clients who have helped me succeed in my amazing journey through life.
Thank you for believing in and supporting me.

But I want to especially thank my parents Thomas Gabor Schiff and Eva Alice Hasko Schiff. They survived the Holocaust as Hungarian revolutionaries and escapees. They were amazing people who gave me confidence, love and a foundation that has guided me my entire life. I love and miss you both every day.

Schiffy

FOREWARD

"Anybody Wanna Make A #78 Drill Bit For The Rest Of Your Life?"

If so, quit reading.

Can you imagine standing at station number three in a tool and grinding shop in the countryside outside St. Louis, Missouri, where your job day-in and day-out is making a #78 drill bit? I mean, that's it. This is what you do for a living. Make this one thing. Every day. All day. Then you go home. Wash, rinse, and repeat.

Well neither could David "Schiffy" Schiff, CEO of The Schiff Group in Washington D.C., and the creative force behind this book.

I mention this because Schiffy brought a crack film crew and shot this very thing for a client video once. I know because I was there. It was my client and I had hired Schiffy's company "Lights, Camera, Action," to help me produce, film, and edit the video for them. They loved it. As far as tool and grinding videos go, it was top of the line in the category and won a couple of niche business marketing awards. Fabulous. I was elated for minutes. It truly was a great video, but — well, tool grinding?

I will always remember this. After the shoot, the crew was striking the sets and moving gear to the vans in the parking lot when Schiffy turns to me and says "You know, God bless these guys for working so hard and doing what they do, somebody has to. But can you imagine doing this day in and day out for the rest of your life? I can't." He meant while he respects anybody who works hard for a living, he set his sights on higher achievements. And there you have it. The nut of this book — more about that in a bit.

It was back in 1990 when Schiffy and I learned we were brothers from different mothers. Neither of us could imagine making #78 drill bits — or anything much like it — as a career path. Not judging. We all do what we do. Yet, our passions guided the both of us to shooting higher in our careers. Far higher. As high as we could go. When you're young and ambitious like we were, it just seemed natural. It's an in-your-blood thing. David has always been an achiever. He's been an actor, a ballet dancer, mountaineer, a drummer, an Emmy Award-winning director, and a filmmaker. He's always been the guy who doesn't settle and keeps reaching for the proverbial brass ring. Only his is gold. And there's more than one.

David and I have been close friends and business associates for some 30 years. After several years of being tight friends and partners in video crime, we went our separate ways in 1993. Schiffy's muse called him to L.A. and then to Washington, D.C. where he worked as an executive in marketing and communications for companies like Boeing, Gannett Government Media, Northrup Grumman Corporation, Booz Allen Hamilton, Aquilent and Jane's Defence Weekly.

I ended up in Minneapolis as Creative Director for two agencies before starting my own in 1999. We lost contact for several years. I got married, and divorced. So did David. Schiffy continued to excel and move up the corporate ladder at these industry-leading companies that supplied the government with a wide range of services, technologies, weapons delivery systems and more. Who would ever have thought it would happen? David surely didn't.

Then about 14 years ago, I was in Washington, D.C., working as a marketing strategy consultant for the U.S. Postal Service. I knew Schiffy didn't live far away in Rockville, Maryland, so I called him before I flew out there, and on the last day of my conference, he picked me up in his truck. Schiffy likes his trucks. He likes long drives and recording messages for work and personal communication. It's his Zen happy place. No anxiety.

As we drove to his house in beautiful suburban Maryland, Schiffy began telling me about his new company, The Schiff Group. It was in its embryonic stages, and he was quite animated and excited to tell me all about the new venture. That evening we went to a Chinese restaurant and talked about the company. At one point I asked what kind of branding he had done when setting up the company and if I could see his website. He looked at me and said "Well, I haven't really thought much about it. I don't have a website." My jaw dropped a bit and I replied, "Are you effin' kidding me? How long have you been in marketing communications?" Then we both had a laugh.

Not long afterwards I got a call from Schiffy. He wanted to hire me to create the Brand Story for The Schiff Group. I eagerly agreed and so began another multi-year journey collaborating with my brother, friend and now client. Using all the tools I had created over the years to help brand Fortune 500 companies; I was able to craft his Brand Story around the central theme of "Let's Change The Conversation."

Why that theme? Schiffy is unique. He doesn't do things like everybody else. He wants to change the way people approach the planning, preparation, and presentation of their offerings to the government. The theme came to me after he explained how he works. How he strives to draw the DNA from his clients to help them find and access the "inner presenter" which lies within each individual's comfort zone —getting to know his clients in depth. He uses a variety of proven psychological and presentation techniques he has mastered throughout his career, to connect with and find compassion for his clients. He aims to inspire them to rise to the occasion under stressful conditions, and to make their business cases and play to what is always a tough room. In effect, to "change the conversation" to each client's favor based on their unique "story" about what they bring to the table. Government evaluators who, it has to be said, are a rather dry and decidedly *not* humorous lot.

To be sure, there are some entrenched competitors in the space The Schiff Group plays in. Fact is the industry is rife with parity. Virtually everyone in this niche market does things the same way they've been done for decades. Boring. Uninspired. Almost by rote. No imagination. No stories to tell. Just requirement boxes being checked and being reliably compliant. But that's about it. There's no soul. No energy. No wow.

That's not good enough for Schiffy. He believes his clients can — and should — be and do better. He is innovative in his philosophy for the work he does and is passionate about one thing at the heart of it: telling a good story. It's what makes the difference and sets his clients apart from their competitors. He helps them change the conversation using all the skills he mastered the past three decades, and be calm and confident doing so.

Now he is bringing his wisdom to you in this book. A collection of compelling stories from his life and career which will make you laugh until you cry. And a few which will make you rethink what you do and how you interact with fellow human beings. The stories he tells in this book are human stories. Stories about his early life, his career, and the people he has helped to overcome obstacles and rise to the occasion when the time calls. To be better at their work than they ever believed was possible.

So, grab some coffee, tea or your favorite adult beverage and dig in. We have designed this book to be non-linear so feel free to open to any chapter and sit back and enjoy.

And if you have to be at station number three in the morning, don't forget to set your alarm. It could be the last day you work there after reading this book.

Steve Penn
Creative Director/Writer

PREFACE

As I began the journey of putting this book together, I often wondered why anybody would want to read it. I mean it's just me. I discussed it with Steve Penn, my dear friend, and the writer of this book, who reminded me of the stories I told him through the years and how people he relayed them to thought they were genuinely interesting. Just to make sure, we shared parts of the book with people who didn't know me, and we were pleasantly surprised to learn, to a person, they really liked what they read. On that positive note, we pushed forward and after more than a year packed with hundreds of hours of interviews, steady, long days spent writing followed by great feedback, rewrites, and a lot of debate, here we are.

It is my sincere hope you will find value beyond the stories I tell here. We all have stories to tell. Are mine more interesting than most? I will leave it to you to decide, but I want you to remember one thing as you read the stories we lay out here: I have never had a plan for my life, I have let my life guide me, and have tried to seize the opportunities which came my way time after time — seemingly out of nowhere.

More than anything, I want to convey in these pages that our lives bring us gifts which arrive to shape us and our future in ways we least expect. They mold our character and move us forward in directions we never could have imagined. I am proud of my accomplishments and experiences. From climbing mountains and watching the Space Shuttle launch alongside NASA engineers, to helping companies win enormous government contracts — and adopting a beautiful baby girl in China. I have seen and done things few people rarely get the opportunity to experience, and for that I am humbly grateful. I truly hope you will find something in these pages to touch you, or help you meet both opportunities and challenges in life head on. Not because you identify with any one story here in this book, but because you will wonder what stories *you* may have in store for yourself if you take the chances which come your way. I will leave you, dear reader, to come up with whatever conclusions seem natural at the end of each chapter. There are no specific lessons or morals to share. Just how one guy overcame his own obstacles to get out there and seize every day he could — and opened himself up to some pretty amazing things in life. I have to say one thing now just to be clear: This book is *not* a self-help or coaching book of any kind. Yes, I am what's called in my profession an Orals Coach. However, I am hoping to simply reveal the human condition as I have experienced it and how my experiences guided me to a comfortable and rewarding place despite suffering from extreme anxiety most of my life. As an adult, I have come to believe anxiety is a far more prevalent condition than most of us will ever know. I didn't really understand what anxiety was until I was formally diagnosed with it in my 50s — so not that long ago. However with help, I came to understand my condition, how to manage it, and how it explained so many things which happened to me. I remember my first anxiety attack came at Sunday School when I was six or seven years old. I hated being there. I remember getting terribly painful, bad stomach aches. Yet my stomach aches got me out of going … and I discovered when I didn't go my stomach aches went away. This would be an experience I relived over and over growing up and well into adulthood. If something didn't "feel" right, I would get bad stomach aches and feel the need to escape from wherever I was. Once I was out of those situations, my pain would go away. As a result of my condition (especially not knowing for so long I even had a condition) I missed out on a lot of things in life. The attacks would come on suddenly whether I was at a concert, a theater shows, on a date, at an outing with friends, or a family get together. My diaphragm would spasm and my upper gastrointestinal tract would get rigid and literally stick out. It was awful and only got worse as I grew older. The symptoms were not just physical. I noticed my personality would change. I desperately tried to close myself in from the outside world and try to find a happy place (within myself) devoid of the horror inside my head. Everyone has a different reaction to anxiety, but this was mine. I would later learn in therapy to control these attacks mentally and emotionally. I learned the cause and was able to take steps to avoid triggering situations and recognize them when they were occurring.

So while I was consciously not trying to control or guide my life so I could leave myself open to whatever came my way, I was secretly fighting to control my own physical and emotional reactions to everything around me. A dichotomy? Absolutely

— and that has never been lost on me. At the end of the day, I was determined not to "settle" for anything. I didn't want the 9-to-5 office job even though I had many. I wanted more. I needed more. It just wasn't me. I wanted to do something in my career and with my life (outside work) which was challenging, different, and difficult. I wanted to meet my opportunities head on and squeeze every ounce of energy and joy from each of them. I wanted to engage life on my own terms and love everything that was happening to me — to be in whatever the moment was. I still do now more than ever. The result has been a lifetime of some really amazing stories, some of which I share with you here today in this book. Perhaps these stories will inspire you to reach for your own brass ring — to take a chance and seize the next opportunity coming your way. Just have the courage to say "yes" and let yourself explore it. That's how we grow. That's how we come to live our lives truly and fully. I also hope you will walk away knowing how important other people are to you and the world you live in. I love people. When my dad used to talk to people on the street, when we were out and about in public, I thought he was nuts. "Why are you bothering these people?" I would ask. "They don't want to talk to you." My father just looked at me one day and said, "Yes, they do. Everybody has stories to tell, they just don't have the opportunity. They are eager to share them if you only give them a chance." Boy, was he right. I have learned so much from so many over the years. Indeed, we all have challenges to overcome, different bridges to cross, paths to walk and enriching stories to live and then tell.

I hope you like the ones I share with you in this book. Not because I'm a famous guy. But because I met those challenges, took those chances, and made my life immensely richer for it. Now it's your turn.

David "Schiffy" Schiff

CHAPTER 1

"High Flights And Deadly Nights."

I was supposed to be an actor. The kid from St. Louis, Missouri who made it to the big time.

But I wasn't going to just be any actor. I was going to be a great actor. Star material in fact. Hell, I was smart and thought I was pretty good looking. Plus, I could dance. I mean, I actually truly was a very good dancer. I could dance like Rudolf Nureyev (in my mind anyway). Surely that would be a bonus, I studied ballet formally. Right?

Umm. No! Reality performed a perfect grand battement and kicked me square in the ass to let me know I was not a great actor. Not even good, really. I was barely okay, at best. That's when I realized I should probably pursue another career.

Like so many of you, my career path to get where I am today was hardly linear. Or planned. Today I own a company which has surpassed my wildest expectations since its inception in 2008. I have flown in one of our country's most sophisticated war planes, been in the bowels of a nuclear submarine, stood next to the most horrific of war machines (ICBM) and stood with the team at NASA to watch the Shuttle launch into space. I have helped some of the world's most advanced and creative minds sell their technology and engineering visions to the DOD and Intelligence communities, and just about every federal government agency seeking contractors to bid on their lucrative contracts. The Schiff Group has been a labor of love — love lost, love found and a love of life. There is so many things about it I have been blessed to experience. I will be sharing some of those stories later in this book.

You will notice a recurring theme as you read this book: Anxiety. I think a lot of people I know personally and professionally would be surprised to know I have struggled with anxiety all my life. It can be a cruel secret people suppress and keep to themselves for fear of appearing different or inadequate. Part of my motivation for writing this book is to let people know they are not alone if they suffer from anxiety. And it's far more commonplace than most people realize. It has plagued me for most of my life, and it's a driving force in all I do when helping my clients understand their fears of presenting are completely normal and there are ways to overcome their struggle when representing their companies in high-pressure, big-money stakes situations. I don't care how intelligent, accomplished or savvy you are, if you have even the slightest sense of anxiety when you are presenting to stone-faced government evaluators in an effort to persuade them to award your company a lucrative satellite or weapons systems contract, your fear of stumbling or making mistakes can be costly. This is where I can help. It's what I do.

However, I think to understand where I am now and how I got here, it's important to know where I came from.

My parents were Hungarian refugees. They met during one of the darkest moments in history after World War II had raged across and ravaged Europe. Hungary had been part of the Axis powers allied with Nazi Germany and later occupied by the Soviet Union. The political leadership of Hungary had adopted oppressive Soviet ideals and practices. People were imprisoned. Tortured. Lynched. By the early 1950s, my parents were in their teens and the political winds were shifting as the people of Hungary grew tired of the repression they had been suffering.

Several years later, in 1956, the people had had enough, and an uprising initiated by university students spilled into the streets of Budapest and other hot spots in the country. The revolution had begun. Fearing the popularity of the revolt and its imminent consequences and potential threat to its power and rule, The Soviet

Red Army invaded Hungary with a massive force and crushed the rebellion in just six days. More than 2,500 Hungarians and 700 Soviet troops were killed in the invasion — some 200,000 Hungarians fled as refugees, most to Austria. Large refugee camps littered the Austrian countryside. Vienna was considered a safe haven and transport and financial assistance was being provided by the Hungarian underground movement to get people across to safety. Then the borders were closed by the military.

Which is where Dad enters the picture.

When the revolution broke out, my dad was a doctor at a hospital in Budapest. By this time, my mom had known my dad for a few years. He would later say she was "very picky" about whom she dated. Mom didn't know at the time but found out soon enough what was going on. It was like something from a Tom Clancy novel. Dad had been transporting money out of Hungary back and forth to aid the resistance and pay off smugglers, along with help from the British Underground. This was done by many in the resistance, but *how* Dad transported the money back and forth was chilling. He drove an ambulance with cadavers filled with cash and gold to hide from checkpoints and random stops. My dad's driving around the country in an ambulance with dead bodies stuffed with much-needed financial help for the resistance, all unknown by my mom. They tried to live an outwardly simple and non-threatening life. She had no idea.

One night they were coming out of a theater during the protests and unrest in Freedom Square and heard gunshots ring out all around them. My dad knew the revolution had begun. The

Russians had learned of the protest plans. They surrounded the protestors and began murdering kids in the streets. It was horrific.

My mother was terrified and told my dad then and there, "We need to leave this country right now!" They had managed to save up a few gold bars which would be their ticket out of war-torn Hungary and over the border into Vienna, Austria, just 150 miles from Budapest. My father said, "Eva, I can't leave just yet and I can't tell you why."

She looked at him and said, "It's over," and stormed off into the night. The next day she and her mother packed some clothes, grabbed a couple of gold bars they had been hiding and headed West across the border into Vienna. They had to pass through a treacherous stretch of countryside known as No Man's Land which was ladened with land mines and heavily patrolled by Soviet soldiers. By chance or by fate (and paying off a smuggler) they managed to make the journey undetected.

Years later my mom would recall feeling a profound sense of relief as they walked into Vienna, and saw a Red Cross flag. They had made it.

Meanwhile, back in Hungary, Dad is still working at the hospital as battles raged around the city. One night he was working in the Emergency Room when a wounded Russian soldier was brought in. My dad, being a physician, had sworn an oath to treat anybody in his care. But shortly after the Russian soldier was brought in, two Hungarian Rebels entered the ER and demanded my father sign a release authorizing the wounded soldier's transfer to another hospital. Dad signed the document, and the soldier was removed from his care. Minutes later, he heard two gunshots. The rebels had taken the wounded soldier behind the building and shot him in the head.

This presented my dad with quite a serious dilemma. He had effectively signed a document which basically allowed a Russian soldier to be executed. He was a wanted man and so he too, escaped to Vienna. But it wasn't over yet.

Years later, I went with my parents to Vienna. They told me stories of what happened next. My dad took me to an old coffee shop in town situated in a small, round courtyard with a fountain across from the opera house. Kind of a storybook, classic European setting. The coffee shop was very long and narrow with a mirror at the very back. My mom was milling around the courtyard as Dad told me to take a seat facing the mirror and to look into the mirror.

"What do you see?" he asked.

"I see Mom," I replied.

"So did I … back on that day when I got to Vienna," he said. "I just happened to be there waiting on a 'delivery' and getting a cup of coffee when I saw your mother. I rushed out to her and begged her to marry me."

"Get away from me, you didn't come with me when you should have," she said to my dad. But after earnest pleading, a heavy heart, and taking a knee, she relented and agreed to marry him. But he had a little news she really didn't want to hear.

"I need to go back to Hungary one more time," he told her. "Let me get your father, and let me get my parents, and then we'll meet you here in a couple of days."

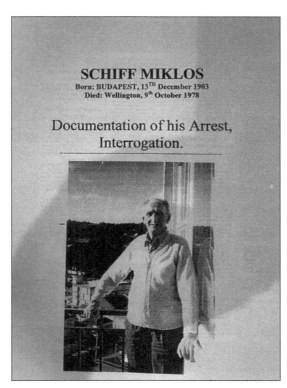

SCHIFF MIKLOS
Born: BUDAPEST, 13TH December 1903
Died: Wellington, 9th October 1978

Documentation of his Arrest,
Interrogation.

Wanting desperately to get her dad out of Hungary, my mom reluctantly agreed. My dad left and immediately upon crossing the border back into Hungary, was arrested. During his absence, they had discovered his method of smuggling using the ambulance. They found the money in the cadavers and some other cash hidden elsewhere.

The Russian command determined he had "authorized" the execution of a Russian soldier, and he was sentenced to be executed — but not until after he had been tortured. Over the next three days, he was hung naked, upside down, had cold water poured on him and was beaten with rubber hoses. He was then thrown in jail. It was December and it was cold. Bitter cold. He knew the next night he was going to be walked out to the edge of the Danube River and shot with a bullet to the head then tossed into the freezing water. A tribute now sits at the spot where the executions took place. It's a small statue of shoes of all shapes, kinds and sizes representing the people who were killed there.

The night before his scheduled execution, the soldier guarding my father had an appendicitis attack and, my dad being a doctor who believed in his oath to heal people, treated him to relieve his pain and symptoms. He did this full well with the memory of what happened to him the last time he tried to treat a Russian soldier. The guard thanked him.

The next day when it was time for him to make his death march to the edge of the Danube, it was a solemn, cloudy morning. As he walked, his mind flashed back to his love Eva. How he missed her and knew they would never be together again. As he took his place in line to be killed, he was stoic. Resolved that this day was the day he would die. Then something happened he never expected. The guard he had treated shot the man in front of him. As it was his turn to take the next bullet, the guard looked at him and said in his husky Russian accent, "I will look other direction. You go."

Not needing a moment to ponder his reversal of fortune, he quickly ran from the river and disappeared into the city. He was alive. He was free. Well, free so far. He made it to the secret location where he had previously hidden "freedom money." He gathered some clothes, pocketed the cash and made way to his parents' house. Once there, he begged his reluctant parents (Miklos and Marika) to come with him to Vienna. To safety. To freedom. They refused to go. He hid a satchel of money in their apartment for them to survive. Failing to convince his own parents to flee with him, he thought about my mom's father. He had promised Eva he would return to her with him where they all would be safe. He left, determined to make good on his promise to his beloved Eva. He arrived at my mom's father's apartment. He needed no convincing to make the dangerous journey with him back across No Man's Land to Vienna, to freedom … and to my mom. They left.

The very next day they arrived in Vienna, to my mother's relieved surprise. They got married that day. I still have the photos they took to etch the moment forever in time, the start of their new life together. Though they were free in Vienna, they wanted to get as far away as possible. My father knew there was a place in America called Camp Kilmer which had been designated as the point of embarkation for U. S. soldiers heading overseas to fight during World War I. He knew it was a safe haven for European refugees fleeing the oppression of Soviet-controlled Hungary.

With the help of freedom supporters, and the Danforth Family, they were sponsored. They flew to the USA, starting their lives and their honeymoon at Camp Kilmer in NJ. My father would learn of his father's arrest in Hungary after he had fled. It seemed if the Soviets couldn't get their man, they would go for his relatives. My grandfather who had survived three concentration camps was abused daily by Nazi soldiers who would smash him in the face with the butt of a rifle. He was tortured and almost killed by Soviet soldiers.

My dad was tried in absentia and found guilty of murder for his role in the death of the Russian soldier. The Soviets sentenced his dad to 12 long years of hard labor. I learned later my father felt tremendous guilt about what had happened to his father because of what he had done. He had nightmares and thought about it all the time.

Once in America, my parents were able to gain sponsorship by the Danforth family. William Danforth had founded the Ralston-Purina company in 1894 in St. Louis, Missouri. He had always felt a strong obligation to help others in need. Danforth would later write a book titled "I Dare You!" in which he described the meaning behind the now world-famous Ralston-Purina checkerboard logo. Its four squares represented a perfectly proportioned balance of the physical, mental, social, and religious aspects of life. This was how life should be lived and he put his money where his mouth was in 1956 when he and other prominent benefactors joined forces to sponsor refugees fleeing Hungary. My Dad was one of them. This is how we ended up in St. Louis.

As is fairly commonplace in the U.S., my father's medical license was not recognized, and he was no longer a doctor in the eyes of the American medical profession because he was from a Communist country. He was crushed but determined to make something of himself. Learning of his situation, the Danforth family made another life-changing contribution to his new life in America: they got him into dental school at the University of Alabama at Birmingham. It was the quickest way to get another degree and utilize many of the skills he had as a doctor in Hungary.

So, in 1959, shortly after I was born, he went to Alabama. While there, he played on the University of Alabama basketball team. Now you have to understand my Dad was 6' 2" and considered tall at the time and had played on the Hungarian national basketball team as a starting center. But that wasn't exactly tall by U.S. standards, and he barely made it as a guard on the team. I still remember seeing his tank top with Alabama blazoned across the top.

At this time, he was taking classes during the day and working nights as an emergency room technician. Dental school was tough for Dad. He didn't speak English and he was failing most everything. But he persevered, learned English, and was able to graduate with a dental degree in two years.

One night while he was working at the hospital, a black man was brought into the ER. As my father began to admit him, an attendant came up to him and said "No, you can't work on him. He needs to go to the colored hospital down the street." My father was shocked. He had escaped torture and near death at the hands of both Nazi and Soviet soldiers. He had managed to flee to the land of the free and the home of the brave. He didn't understand why there were "whites only" fountains and restaurants. It blew his mind. Remember, this was at the very beginning of the civil rights movement, and Alabama was hardly a bastion of tolerance. That's when he decided to join the Air National Guard. He wanted to repay the country for giving him his freedom. He served as a flight surgeon for 30 years and retired. He was a proud man and proud of its ideals. He would take me to Blues hockey and Cardinal baseball games, and when the national anthem played, he stood tall and would sing it out at the top of his lungs. Really loud. I remember thinking it was the most embarrassing thing in the world.

So from humble beginnings as a Nazi concentration camp survivor, a member of the Hungarian Resistance, and cheating certain death at the hands of the Soviets, to a life of service to his new country, my father showed me what loyalty, strength, and passion are. What being tough and determined is all about. About the will to live. My Dad was a tough son of a bitch though. He used his voice like a riding crop. It stung every time he spoke. He was a very loving man but was a really bad communicator. We had a super tough love-hate relationship.

Like most kids, I didn't appreciate all of this until I learned all about it later in my life. To this day, I am proud of him and what he accomplished in arguably the most difficult, trying times any human could possibly endure. When Dad passed a few years ago, my mom asked me if I could arrange a military flyover with

F-16s. By this time, I was well established in my career, which afforded me many opportunities to work closely with the military and Department of Defense at the highest levels. Several of those stories are on the pages which follow.

When I told her I didn't have that kind of power, she scoffed, assured I could make it happen. On the day of the funeral, it was very solemn and eerily silent as the Honor Guard began to play taps.

That's when a miracle occurred. Out of the blue an F-16 from a nearby McClellan Air Force Base flew directly over the grave site. It was a complete coincidence. My mother was stunned. Just floored. She turned to me breathlessly and said, "How did you do that, David?"

I smiled at her and said simply, "I've got my ways."

CHAPTER 2

"Goodbye Bullies. Hello Detroit Rock City."

After the war, my parents, like so many Jewish refugees from all across Europe, looked to America as their beacon of hope and possibility for a new and better life [in this great country]. They eventually settled in St. Louis, Missouri, where I was born. By both the times then and today's standards, anyone would consider my upbringing to be fairly privileged. We lived in Clayton, a suburb of St. Louis that was by all accounts upscale and affluent. I grew up in a loving yet fairly conservative household. My father was, without question, the king of the household. My mom was the peacemaker and arbiter.

To Schiffy
Rock + Art
Forever !

I was taught to be thoughtful, kind and independent. Rules were important. So were truth, honor, and personal responsibility. Although my childhood was relatively normal and insulated from the problems and issues so many families faced in the turbulent '60s, something inside of me never felt quite right. I felt different and it was more than being Jewish in a gentile world. I never felt in control. I had a lot of self-doubt. I would later come to understand this was the beginning of what would become a lifelong battle with anxiety, something I struggle with to this very day. I'll be addressing it in various ways throughout this book.

I never fully applied myself well enough in my school studies. My grades stunk and there were reasons for that: undiagnosed anxiety and being bullied. In middle school I began to get bullied, which, along with what I now know was anxiety, severely affected and influenced my self-image and my life in general. I was apprehensive, actually downright afraid to go to school. I never knew when I was going to get shoved into the bathroom, beat up, taunted, teased and ridiculed. It was a very rough time for me. Looking back, I feel as though I was in "Survivor" mode for most of that time. In a word, it was awful. And very painful.

Prior to seventh grade, I had a few minor brushes with bullies. There was a kid in grade school who used to make me give him my ice cream sandwich for lunch. He would just say "Give that to me. I want it." And I would. I just didn't know how to handle those kinds of situations. I was engaged in one fight, and I lost. Badly. The kid hit me once in the ear and I cried and ran home to my mom. That was about it at the time. I kept to myself and just did my best to fit in. The remainder of my grade school years were fairly uneventful.

Then I got to junior high school. In seventh grade there was a group of people who were the "cool kids" … or so they thought and acted. I realized very quickly I just didn't fit in. I literally looked and dressed differently. I would wear slacks or corduroys and everybody else was wearing jeans and oxfords. And there was so much socially I didn't know and things I didn't have which other kids did. When I would ask my parents about getting this or that, I was told sternly no, I cannot have those things. What's more, I didn't need them. Frugality was a trait among a lot of

Jewish families because of the Holocaust. They did without most of the non-essentials other families had and enjoyed.

The 45-minute bus ride to junior high school was long, and I dreaded it every time I got on the bus. I have since learned in talking with other people who dealt with some of the same things I did that busses were just a bad place for the misfit kids. It's a closed space. It's an easy place to get cornered and picked on. I would see other kids get bullied by the troublemakers. One kid was pushed off the bus and his schoolbooks were tossed down the sewer. It was awful and it terrified me. I also had my books thrown away or stolen, which only served to make getting good grades all the harder.

The other terrible place for me was the boy's bathroom. I would be followed into the bathroom where I would get hit, smacked and pushed around. The bad kids could be brutal and incredibly mean. Urinating on me. I had my head stuck into the toilet. It was disgusting and it was killing me inside. If you've ever been bullied, you know what it can do to your psyche. If you haven't, consider yourself lucky. No kid should ever have to go through that.

It only got worse when I was in high school. The cast of characters were the same but more experienced at their malicious craft; they had refined the art of making kids like me feel like shit. And the laughing — the laughing echoed through my mind. It was a lot like the scene in the Stephen King movie "Carrie" where there was a swirl all around me of people laughing and pointing at me in what seemed like slow motion. All of them drunk in their perverse, crazy carnival of behavior — sneering, ridiculing, and taunting me. It haunted me for years in subtle and not-so-subtle ways.

I did the best I could. I knew I would never fit in. When it came to music, they liked Marshall Tucker and Charlie Daniels. I liked Led Zeppelin and KISS. (Little did I know what impact KISS made on me. More about that shortly.) And sports? Not so much. I eventually became a very good hockey player and I loved going to see the St. Louis Blues play at Kiel Auditorium.

With all the bullying and badgering, my dad was concerned for my safety and recommended I learn karate to defend myself.

What a total disaster that was. Then one day something wild happened. I think it was my sophomore year and I had watched this movie called "The Doberman Gang." It had come out a few years earlier in 1972 and it was about a talented dog trainer who taught six Doberman Pinschers to rob a bank. He named the dogs after famous bank robbers John Dillinger, Bonnie, Clyde, Pretty Boy Floyd, Baby Face Nelson, and Ma Barker.

I thought that was crazy, but it led me to have a crazy idea myself. I was going to get myself a Doberman and sic him on the bullies. No, seriously. That was the plan, and so I did. in fact, did get a Doberman, and I named him Sir Marcus Alan Dillinger following in the movie's footsteps. My parents showed me the photo of my new pup's father. Of course, my dog was just a pup, but I cooked up another crazy idea that effectively served as my first foray into the world of marketing. I spread a rumor that I was going to seek revenge against the bullies by unleashing my personal hound from Hell on them all.

I took a photo of Dillinger's sire — an, imposing full-grown dog who weighed 110 pounds, to school telling people payback is coming and it's coming in the form of a new attack dog I had trained to recognize and put bullies in their place.

One day I took Dillinger to school. He was only six or seven months old at the time. One of the bullies, a guy named Potter, confronted me in the hallway and said, "Oh, is this the dog that's supposed to attack me?" As he was laughing, I said, "Well, not now, but eventually, when he grows up." And he said, "Oh, he's not grown?" I showed him the picture, and just for a moment that's seared into my memory forever, he got defensive. He even looked a little scared. At that moment — that magical moment — I felt for the first time I was actually in a better place than he was. I gained new-found confidence.

I still was not performing well in school. So much so my father suggested I learn karate. I just wasn't into it. It didn't feel right to me. I wasn't a fighter. I was more into the arts and doing creative things. This was the place where I felt safe to express myself. I wanted to act. I wanted to express myself in ways which would make me feel good about myself. Something to give me validation. So, I found other kids who were more like me, including Louis Schwarz who remains to this day one of my dearest friends.

Louis and I and a couple other "unpopular" kids hung out. We rode bikes. We took summer trips together, and we used our collective skills and creativity to construct our own little world. We were not cool, and we didn't care. We even developed a comic book and a movie series called "Strange Versus Normal". Strange was an acronym which meant Supreme Team Retaliatory Agents Nemesis Guarding Earth. And normal was the Nincompoop Organization of Retarded Morons Against Law. (Couldn't do that today of course) All of us were strange. All of the bullies were normal. We loved this new world.

But while I had found shelter in this new safe haven of friendship and fantasy, my grades still sucked. My parents were concerned. My Dad thought I was intellectually challenged. After all, he had done all he could to give me a good education, but I wasn't performing well. That's when something really wild happened; something which would open doors I thought were forever closed. My father had arranged for me to take a test at school with the guidance counselor. Now, taking tests at school was pretty normal, so I thought nothing of it. Take your No. 2 lead pencil, answer the questions and hand it in. Just like you would with any test or assignment. About a month later, I got called to the counselor's office. To my surprise, both of my parents were there. I freaked out a bit and asked, "What are you guys doing there?"

"Don't worry about them," said the counselor. Looking directly at me he said, "David, do you know why you're here?" And I said, "Um, I guess. I don't know, something about that test you gave me a little while back?"

"Yes," he replied dryly. Still looking at me with a serious face, he asked me, "How do you think you did?"

With a bit of a snarky tone I replied back equally dryly, "I passed it?" At that point my Dad was champing at the bit and blurted out, "Well, is my son okay?" wanting to know if I was indeed intellectually challenged.

"Uh, no, Dr. Schiff, your son is hardly challenged. As a matter of fact, he scored insanely high."

I had been given an IQ test. And I had scored the highest in my age group in Missouri state history. I was, in fact, a candidate for MENSA. If you're not familiar, MENSA is the largest and oldest high-IQ society in the world. It is a non-profit organization open to people who score at the 98th percentile or higher on a standardized, supervised IQ or other approved intelligence test.

It was official. I was a pretty damned smart kid.

But, true to form, my Dad said, "Well, why are his grades so bad?" Before the counselor could answer, I just started talking about the bullying. The prevailing thought back in those times was that bullying wasn't an issue. You took some boxing classes, bucked up and fought back or just suffered through it. You didn't try to report them because word would get out and you'd just be far worse off than you were before. But armed with the proof that I was smarter than most all of them, I chose to suffer through it. The wheels in my head began to turn, I was wondering, maybe I would be okay in the end.

The bullying continued, but I had grown accustomed to it. I immersed myself in this new world and in the world of theater, the arts in general and music. Sweet music saved me in a lot of ways.

Music was something I could enjoy all by myself. I was looking for outlets to heal my hurt and lift my spirits. A place to escape to and be me — a refuge from the hell I was enduring socially just about every day. That's when rock and roll entered my life. One day my sister and I were sitting in my room doing homework and listening to the radio, K-SHE 95, the local classic rock station and they were playing a song called "Rock And Roll All Night And Party Every Day" by a band called KISS.

Something about that song hit me like a proverbial ton of bricks. My sister noticed me grooving to the tune and said, "Oh, you like that?" I said, "Yeah. I love it." She started laughing. Now you have to understand my sister was actually two years younger than I was but was always more mature. She acted like she was 30. So she said, "Those are the guys you call fags because they wear makeup." Now you have to understand the times. Today that word is understandably offensive, but in the mid '70s, the word, at least to me, meant effeminate but not gay. That was my understanding then.

The next day after school, I ran down to Almar Village Music which was the cool music store in St. Louis and bought "Alive," the first record by KISS. I was completely captivated by the cover. The smoke, lights, and costumes. Gene Simmons with his tongue out and the little candelabra sitting off to the side. I had never seen anything like it. I remember eagerly putting it on the turntable and as I listened, I felt alive inside. I had never heard that kind of energy in music ... and it was live.

Now you have to remember I was raised very conservatively. But here's something kind of weird and funny. Before this, when

I was 15, my Dad had bought me my first two rock albums "The Partridge Family Tree Album" and the Osmond Brothers record "One Bad Apple." Now, at the risk of being canceled by true rock snobs, I really loved Donnie Osmond. I thought he was really cool. A kind of hip, popular teenager, exactly my age. We had similar hair. So, with that as my "rock" background, imagine how I was blown away when I heard KISS and their level of crazy, live energy with explosions and all of the fire and madness going on. The next day, I was listening again to KISS on the radio and at the end of the song there was an announcement KISS would be performing live in concert on Halloween Night at Kiel Auditorium (where The St. Louis Blues hockey team played — more on my passion for hockey later). KISS on Halloween Night? Perfect. I immediately rushed down to Peach's Records And Tapes where they sold concert tickets and camped overnight to get my tickets. I'll never forget that concert as long as I live. Bob Seger and Natural Gas opened the show. When the lights came on, KISS took the stage amid fire belching to the sides and behind them, smoke billowing out. I was transported to another world. It just blew my mind. It was non-stop energy for the entire show.

Being a KISS fan wasn't exactly cool, either. I got hassled for that as well. It seems I remember when I graduated from high school, I was walking up to get my diploma and somebody in the audience yelled, sneered really, "Hey, KISS!" which was meant as an insult as I was called KISS by some of the bullies. Here I was listening to this amazing rock music and thinking it was cool while all the "cool" kids were laughing at me AND the band. Everybody thought KISS were "fags" back then. "Who wears makeup and lipstick?" they said? "It's stupid," they said. I couldn't win.

The beautiful, sweet irony is later in life, just a few years ago, I would become friends with Paul Stanley aka Starchild, the lead singer and rhythm guitarist for KISS. I actually had the chance to tell him about this when we first met. He just put his hand on my shoulder and said, "Schiffy, you'd be amazed at how many people in life would bully KISS fans just because they liked us because we were different and wore makeup. We weren't typical."

I can't tell you how much that meant to me. It was validation. It was release in a lot of ways. Here I am a successful entrepreneur who started and built a very successful company, finally feeling free of so much of those bad times because my hero was just like me. I always wanted to be somebody unique and different and expand on my skills. I loved this band for being exactly that. It was literally music to my ears.

I didn't realize how much what Potter and the other bullies did affected me. It wasn't until years later and with the amazing help of a therapist who has helped to change my life, that I realize the totality of those days; memories came flooding back.

I remembered in my senior yearbook, where you could write a little paragraph beneath your photo, I wrote that I hoped these people get what's coming to them. I then listed the initials of all the people who had hurt me in high school. Years later my sister would say, "Boy, if you had done that today you'd probably get arrested."

Maybe so. But it felt good at the time. I have learned that closure is a journey, not a destination, and 15 years after I graduated from high school, I was at a St. Louis Blues hockey game. As I sat down, I turned to my side and sitting next to me was … Potter. I was stunned and became quite uneasy. He looked at me and said, "Oh my God, David Schiff, how are you?"

I was stunned as I thought, "How the fuck do you think I am asshole?"

Through my maturity and therapy I had come to realize bullies very often have no recollection of their actions or deny the behavior which so deeply affects the targets of their reprehensible attacks. I waited a moment as anxiety once again washed over me. "How am I supposed to act right now in this moment?" I asked myself. We made small talk when Potter said, "Is something wrong?"

I turned to him and said, "You really don't have any idea, do you?" And he said no. So I suggested we go to Tom's Bar and Grill to talk. We ordered some burgers, and I poured my heart out to him. I could tell he felt pretty bad about what he was hearing from me as he hung his head, shook it a couple of times, and apologized to me. He was kind enough about it. But for me? For me it was still there. Better, but still there in the old memory chip.

Years later, my best buddy Louis Schwartz and I went to our 20th high school reunion. As we arrived, I saw a girl I had a crush on back in the day. Her name was Judy. She was so attractive in school and even more beautiful there at the reunion. I approached her demurely and said hello. We chatted for a few minutes, and I learned she was married. I asked her if we could take a picture and she let our photo be taken with my arm around her, which I had always wanted to do but had been impossible. She was always nice, but she was part of the "cool" kids' group and I smiled as the photo was snapped.

I mingled throughout the room and engaged in some small talk with some of my former classmates. Several of the bullies were there. Married with kids and talking about their lives. As the conversation turned to reflection on our high school years, they laughed about this or that. As the reminiscing turned to me, I said simply, "I don't think you guys realize how bad it was for me." As they listened, I continued with a bit of what I had experienced and ended by saying, "I only hope that what happened to me never happens to your kids."

As I left, I realized this was probably as close to closure as I would ever get. All of those terrible experiences shaped who I am today. I have learned to take care of myself and not rely on other people as much as I may have wanted to earlier in my life. To make my own way.

While there is no longer deep anger, the hurt is still there a bit. Then there wasn't this thing called therapy. At least I didn't know there was. Today, with help from friends, colleagues and mental health professionals, I have been able to turn those bad memories into life lessons, and today I enjoy people from all walks of life. I can trust. I can empower others and I can always know deep down that when something bad happens, I can rely on myself to get through it. And, yes, with the help of all the truly great people I have in my life right now.

And KISS still fucking rocks!

CHAPTER 3

"Paging Dr. Schiff …"

I was raised to have a strong work ethic from a very early age. Like so many kids, I had a paper route until I was 15 years old. I hated it. So much so I eventually let papers pile up without delivering them. I worked a few odd jobs here and there. Once I tried my hand at selling stereo systems at a local music store. A friend of my father's worked there. Dad introduced me to the guy, and he said, "So, you want to sell stereo systems, eh?"

I shrugged my shoulders and said, "Not really, but I'm here."

He laughed and said, "Okay, sell me a stereo," he said.

So, without thinking, I said, "Can I help you with anything?"

Without hesitation, he said, "Well you fucked that up." I said, "How did I do that? What do you mean?"

"Let me show you how it's done," he said. He walked over and then asked ME to pretend to be a customer looking at a system. I said okay and played along. He started his spiel with, "That's some super cool equipment you're looking at." Playing the role, I said, "Yeah it really is."

"So," he asked, "what kind of music do you like?"

"Led Zeppelin," I replied dryly.

He left and came quickly back with a Led Zeppelin 8-track tape (yes, an 8-track), put it in the system and said, "Check this out."

"Wow," I said. "That's amazing." I was truly impressed. He showed me some of the features and by the time his pitch was done I was ready to buy damn near everything in the store. He was good. After we left, I kept thinking about all he said to me about selling.

While I didn't want that particular job, I learned something that would help me later in marketing and sales. Don't do a close-ended pitch. Don't make it a yes or no, black or white proposition. Get in their heads and figure out what moves them. My friend Steve Penn once told me he learned a similar lesson. He worked closely with some top salespeople at his company who told him you can't really "sell" anybody something. But you CAN make somebody want to buy. And that is exactly right.

Other odd jobs included a one-day stint at a restaurant. Hated it. I was a runner and once while bringing out an order I ate a couple olives off the tray because I was hungry. I was fired on the spot. For a week I was a bagger at a big local grocery store. I was bagging up some eggs for this old lady and she started bitching at me about how I wasn't doing it right. I looked at her and told her what she could do with her eggs. End of that job.

One day, my father said, "Why don't you just get a job at the hospital?" He was the head of the Oral and Maxillofacial Surgery department at Jewish Hospital in St. Louis and was well-liked and respected. I thought about it, and one day went to the hospital and met with somebody in administration, most likely human resources, but I didn't know about those things. After some discussion, they decided to start me off doing some orderly work. I was basically a gofer and did odd jobs and even some janitorial work. But I did a good job and was treated very well. After all, I was Dr. Schiff's kid and there were high expectations. I liked being there. I got to meet people I really respected and was learning a lot about how a hospital works.

As I got to know the staff, nurses, and physicians, I got more involved helping them. Stuff you probably wouldn't be allowed to do today. Even being there while patients were being worked on. I ended up spending a lot of time in the ER. I saw a lot. One thing I learned about myself was that I have a high degree of empathy for people in pain. I saw it first-hand, and it bothered me deeply to see suffering. I cried when others weren't looking. I came to realize viscerally and up close and personal how skillful and dedicated the people who work in hospitals really are. It touched me and made a big impression, and I think that is when I first realized helping people is a good and noble thing to do. I always felt for the patients and saw how these hospital heroes helped them. One day I was discussing this with an ER doctor and asked him how he does this day in and day out. He told me you can have compassion, but you can't get involved with patients too personally or you will lose perspective. You're there to do your job, period. It kind of shocked me, to be honest. But as time went on, I began to understand what he meant. It's funny, because as hard and rugged as my Dad could be, he had a different take on all of that. He always believed it would be good for doctors to take a course in interpersonal dynamics because he thought some doctors are just too "cold" and don't realize how scared their patients can be. He came to that realization after having been a patient himself in that hospital years before.

As I continued working there, I wasn't really doing too much and just looked forward to getting free cheesy fries from the cafeteria. It all changed a few days later when I was "drafted" into action. A man had been brought into the ER with an irregular heartbeat. He was probably in his late 50s and didn't look so great. At the time the way they treated was using the paddles you rub together to jolt a person's heart — so it changed the rhythm and got it beating properly. I was right there, and the attending doc told me to hold the guy's hand.

The doctor rubbed the gel on the paddles, held them over his chest and said, "Clear" and then zapped him. The guy's chest jumped out and there was this kind of "Ooof" sound he made that scared the hell out of me. I had never seen such a thing in real life, just on the TV show *Emergency*. I thought we were hurting the guy, but the doc assured me it was just a muscle reaction.

After the doc finished with him, I came back into his room and his family was with him. He thanked me for being so kind and holding his hand. It was kind of surreal.

One time, I got to suture and dress a wound. I had seen this done several times during my time at the ER. But doing it myself? That was a first. Some young woman had stepped on a broken bottle in Forest Park, just across the street from the hospital. She came into the ER and the doc inspected her wound carefully. He cleaned it out and proceeded to check to see if anything was cut or broken. Then he asked the nurse to bring him a syringe with a painkiller. He swabbed her foot clean with a little alcohol and cotton, then injected her between her big and second toes. After a few minutes he asked her if she felt anything. She said she didn't. He began examining her wound. She was cut pretty wide and deep. He found her tendon and checked it to see if it was damaged. He asked if she could move her foot up and down as he gently held onto the tendon. She said yes. That's when things got weird for me.

"You want to feel it?" he asked me? "What?" I replied. He told me to put on gloves and I came over. He guided my hand so that my finger could feel her tendon. He told the young lady she was going to be just fine. Then he looked at me and said "Okay, David, you've seen how this works. Why don't you go ahead and suture this up."

Now, he had shown me how to do this and I had watched him a few times by now. But do it myself? He instructed me what to do. He handed me the suture material and the hemostats. He guided me through each stitch until I was done and then walked me through how to tie it off. After I was done, he said, "Great job," told the patient she was going to be just fine and left the room.

The next story I want to tell really shook me up — badly. A woman had been rushed to the hospital and as she came in, I saw one hand was wrapped up and bulky. It almost looked like it was in a boxing glove. She was probably in her 30s and appeared very distressed. Her chest was also completely wrapped. As she was wheeled in, I heard loud yelling and a lot of commotion coming from the lobby. I went down to see what it was and, as it turns out, it was her husband. Apparently, he was very drunk and was screaming at everybody in the lobby. Security was called to go down and get things under control.

Meanwhile, the woman was taken in for X-rays on her chest. Things were pretty tense; at least it was for me. When the X-rays came back, the on-call ER surgeon, who was a friend of my Dad, called me in as he was looking at the X-rays pinned up on the lights in the dark room. Dad had been trying to teach me how to read them at the time, so I guess it was timely. I took a look and said, "Okay, little Schiffy. What do you see?"

As I peered up at the light board, I saw the X-rays for her hand and her chest. The chest X-ray was covered all over in tiny white dots. "I think those are bad X-rays. There are white dots all over it."

"No," said the surgeon. "The X-rays are shocking."

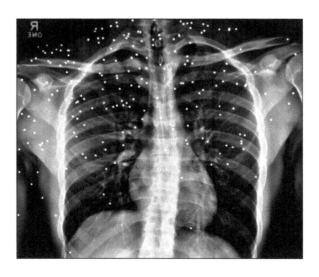

I didn't understand. He then explained the back story. The woman had been at her house with her kids when her husband came home extremely drunk. He was mumbling incoherently and was upset about the kids being too noisy. Apparently, he had grabbed a loaded shotgun and approached the woman who put her hand over the barrel. He pulled the trigger which pierced the flesh of her hand between her thumb and forefinger causing the bullet pellets to scatter all over inside her upper torso. The surgeon pointed to the X-rays and told me to take a closer look. I leaned in and looked as he said, "Not one of those pellets penetrated a vital organ. Those white spots you see are the pellets embedded in her chest cavity and upper body. All of them lodged in soft tissue."

I was stunned. I asked how they're going to get all of those out.

"We won't," he replied. "It would be more dangerous to do multiple surgeries, so they will stay there unless a vital organ is threatened."

I nodded and then he joked, "But she may have an issue with metal detectors."

Those were some of the stories about the ER, but I want to recount one last memory from the time I was moved up to the surgical suites. I thought this was very cool because I would scrub up just like the nurses and docs and I began assisting them in actual operations. One of the things I would do is hold up the retractor to keep the skin open while the doctors worked inside the patients. I would also help by using little sponges to sop up blood around the surgery area. I got to assist in everything from brain surgery to spinal surgery to a heart valve replacement and a hip replacement. I remember the hip replacement was brutal. It looked like carpentry to me. First you tear and pull back the hip skin and muscle to expose the ball and socket joint. They would then separate them, saw off the ball joint and replace it with a synthetic ball joint, hammer it into place and then put everything back together.

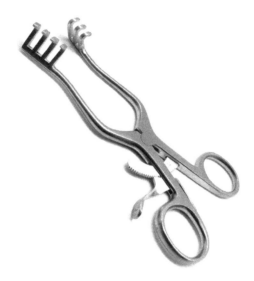

I thought, "Yeah, I could see myself doing all of that."

Yeah. None of that happened. That was the end of my "medical" career.

I was ready to be an actor.

CHAPTER 4

"A Different Kind Of Star Is Born."

I was always fascinated by TV and the movies. Just the visual medium in general. The idea of "moving pictures" fascinated me as a kid. How emotions, ideas, and concepts could be communicated through a combination of the expressions on people's faces and the tone and tenor of their voices and actions. I was born in 1959 and grew up in the 60s — the "Golden Age" of television. It was a magical time.

Think about the eras I've lived through: I watched a man landing on the moon, I grew up with Walter Cronkite, I watched black and white television convert into color, and I saw live television change over to sitcoms and series like Marcus Welby MD. I remember my mother telling me when she saw the Wizard of Oz the first time in a theater, there had never been a color movie before — and when Dorothy opened up the door after her house had landed in Oz and you saw color, it was an amazing directorial style. Slowly unveiling the door as she walked out of the house to unveil the stunning, beautiful place was magical. To this day my favorite movie is the Wizard of Oz, and my favorite song is "Somewhere Over The Rainbow." I always get emotional hearing it. As a funny aside I was with my family in Hawaii on the Big Island on the Kona side and there was a ukulele shop. The guy who owned the shop was from Virginia. He was kind of an older guy with a white beard, but he played a mean ukulele. He played "Somewhere Over The Rainbow" for my daughter Kira who was absolutely mesmerized by it. We bought a ukulele for her, and to this date she still plays string instruments. That moment in Hawaii meant something special to her.

Beyond the attraction of what eventually gets presented "on the screen," I was just as intrigued by the process of getting it there. The technical aspects of filmmaking from behind the lens and the camera. The art of capturing the action, going into post-production to carefully edit what the film had captured, and try to create a moving story of what each frame was communicating. I have always had a great respect for the art of filmmaking in all of its forms.

My interest in film and the process of making films came to fuller fruition when I was in high school. Now, as I've said before, I was and still am a nerd about stuff like this. I can geek out pretty quickly and do pretty deep dives into the technology of it all.

In school, I was "that guy" — the classic projection room nerd. Back then, a projection room was outfitted with a 16-millimeter projector. I got my editing chops by actually razor blading and scotch taping pieces of film together.

But even before that, I had played around with ideas with my dear friend Louis Black. Back then, Louis had already been well into the whole filmmaking thing. He was an excellent animator who used whatever was at his disposal to create all kinds of stuff related to film and movies. It was a really cool time in both of our lives, and we loved making shit up on the fly. At this time Star Wars was crazy big, and we were blown away by the special effects. In fact, we tried our own hand at homemade special effects. Using 8mm film, we would try to replicate light sabers by taking a magnifying glass, Clorox bleach and a needle, and etching out a wooden dowel rod which created a really cool rainbow effect.

We'd make a model using stop motion. Move the rod an inch and click a frame. Move it another inch and click another frame and so on, it was painstaking work. People probably would think it was boring and we were crazy. Hell, we didn't care. We enjoyed it and we learned a lot through trial and error. We did a lot of experimental things with film trying to be creative. It provided us with great joy and was a nice escape from the pressures of being the "uncool" kids in school.

We'll talk more about film a bit later in this story. But I want to get back to acting for a moment. I still had the acting bug. It was strong and growing stronger all the time. Now, I had grown up being classically trained in the arts. I took piano lessons for many years. I also moved into voice, and I played trumpet in grade school. I also took ballet and dancing lessons for several years. The stage was calling, and I wanted to be ready. So music and theater were always a very big part of my life growing up. Now remember that my father was a lieutenant colonel in the 131st Tactical Air Command Wing at Lambert Field in St. Louis. He was a flight surgeon. He always wanted me to be in a noble profession — a lawyer or a doctor. Preferably a doctor and possibly even taking over his practice one day. Something he would be proud of. In fact, at just 16 years of age, I was working at Jewish Hospital as a retractor holder and a technician of sorts in the ER, which made my Dad proud. So after high school I enrolled at University of Missouri — St. Louis (UMSL) in a pre-med curriculum. I wanted so much to please him and make him proud of his son.

But I couldn't stop thinking about movies and the theater. However, grades again were an issue. At the end of my first semester at UMSL, my collective GPA was a miserable .5. Yes, you read that right: a .5. Think of the movie "Animal House." That was me. During my second semester, I had to take an elective course and I chose "Introduction To Theater." One of the requirements of the course was to audition for a part in the main school show and if you got the part, you got an automatic "A" for the class. That would go a fair way to helping my abysmal GPA. So I auditioned and, to my great joy and surprise, I got one of the leading roles.

The play was called "The Rimers of Eldritch" by Lanford Wilson, who was a Missouri playwright. I played Josh Johnson. I'll never forget that part. I remember the whole process of rehearsals and learning the lines — and eventually doing the show and what that did for my self-esteem and confidence. My first theater Professor was a guy named Denny L. Bettisworth. Denny had salt and pepper hair and a salt and pepper beard. He smoked Lucky Strikes. Back then you could smoke in the classroom. He was a character, a truly classic thespian. He also ran the Theater Department at the university.

One day in class he was discussing avant-garde or contemporary theater, and somebody in class said, "Oh, that sucks." He paused, turned to the student and said "Pablo Picasso" and began to tell the class a story. As the story goes, Pablo Picasso was at an art exhibit in New York, and people were milling around. Some walked up to him dripping with star-struck enthusiasm. "We are such big fans of your work, sir," and "We just love your stuff." Picasso, being uncharacteristically patient, was nice about it all. He looked across the room and saw a woman staring at one of his paintings for quite some time.

He wanders over to her and says, "Uh, excuse me, ma'am", to which she replies, "Oh, Mr. Picasso, I'm such a huge fan of your work."

"Oh, thank you," he replied. "I appreciate that, but I noticed you've been staring at this one painting of mine for quite some time, and I was wondering why."

The woman says, "Well, I don't mean to offend, but I was raised a staunch Catholic, and this painting, the rendition of the Madonna, to me distorts the natural beauty of the Virgin Mary, and I find it troubling."

Being as gracious as he can, he begins a discussion with the woman about family, each of them sharing stories with one another. The woman then reaches into her purse and retrieves a photograph of her family to show him. Picasso looks at the photograph intently and then says to her dryly, "Well, it's a lovely family, but are they really that small?"

The whole class laughed. We got it. Boom. Mind blown. When I heard the story, it made me realize what perspective was really all about. That story gave me something which made my mind quite happy with how it was not how others expected it be. Having a high IQ is not without its drawbacks. Social awkwardness. Fear of being yourself. Anxiety about what others think of you because you are, well, "different". Having been bullied most of my life had taken its toll on my self-esteem and had exacerbated my already deeply ingrained sense of social awkwardness and anxiety. But there and then, because of my love for television, film and acting, I knew my brain was just fine. I could be high functioning in many different ways — knowing there is no such thing as right or wrong when it came to creativity and my ability to express myself in several different avenues. Now, of course, directors have their feelings about what's right and wrong in any given performance, and I immediately turned my interest to directing. Even though I loved acting and had done stand-up comedy for a time, I immersed myself in learning all about directing as well as acting. But acting still burned brightly inside my soul and was my top priority.

By this time I had switched my major to theater but had not told my father. My grades shot up and I even made the Dean's List. But as I was still living at home, all my mail went to our family mailbox, including a letter announcing I had gone from probation to the Dean's List. My father opened the letter and as he was congratulating me, he noticed the header on the letter said

Office of Speech Communication, he had enrolled me in Pre-Med. He got angry, and we had what would be one of many arguments about my career path. As a survivor of the Holocaust, my dad had strict and narrow views of success. You can be a doctor, you can be a lawyer, or you can be a ditchdigger. That was it. So even though I had been immersed in dance, theater and music, the concept of it ever becoming a profession was the furthest thing from my father's mind. All my father really ever wanted was for me to be successful; yet his definition of successful and mine were very different. This started what was a rather tumultuous relationship between the two of us, with lots of screaming back and forth. I know now more than anything that my father just wanted me to do well. But owing to his strict upbringing, he had his own anger issues — a difficult relationship with his father. When his parents refused to go with him to Vienna, they ended up getting prosecuted and going to jail for 12 years. It was not my Dad's fault, but Russians were brutal and regularly go after the next of kin and punish them. He carried that guilt with him. I soon came to know he just wanted me to succeed in America and avoid the horrors he had to endure.

When I graduated college, I made a big decision to head to LA with the dream of becoming that great actor I talked about earlier. You know, the St. Louis kid who made it to the big time. I would learn I really was far from it. In fact, I was a miserable failure. After about a year I realized my acting dream was never going to pan out, I decided to come back home to St. Louis to see if I could fare any better behind the camera.

After looking around for opportunities, I got my first job at KETC, the PBS affiliate in St. Louis on channel 9. I started doing some camera work, but I also appeared now and then on camera for the pledge drives — reporting the tallies for the fundraising efforts. Not exactly Hollywood, but I learned a lot. Around that same time, I had started doing camera work for the St. Louis Cardinal baseball games. I loved it. I was a huge hockey and baseball fan, so this was right up my alley. As the months went on, I expanded my technical knowledge and soon was in the mobile production truck directing remotely. I was hungry to learn all I could. I immersed myself in every aspect of the business. Production, lighting, stagecraft.

This is when I joined the IBEW, The International Brotherhood of Electrical Workers and International Alliance of Theatrical Stage Employees (IATSE) in St. Louis. These two unions covered everything electrical for television, and everything stagehand for the theater and huge productions. It was these two unions that supported all the live production in Saint Louis. I was able to work concerts as a roadie; work baseball games as a cameraman, editor and slow-motion replay specialist; and ultimately an assistant director for live television for the Cardinals baseball team, the Saint Louis Blues hockey team, and the Saint Louis indoor soccer franchise.

I think what I found so interesting about union work and lots of the people I met was it was always about the next project; it was always about the work, and always about being brothers to each other. I felt my independence was limited, and I also I could be the one who was supervising all these people versus the guy that was being one of those people. The good news is when you are in any industry the best way to learn is to do the jobs of the people that will ultimately work for you—I believe it makes you a better boss. During my time at the arena in St. Louis and Kiel auditorium, I had the profound luck of supporting the greatest rock and roll bands of all time as a roadie. I would get a call from the union boss and go down to the hall we were supporting. I would get my assignment—which could include everything from unloading or loading a truck, rigging cables and support chains, hanging the trusses that held the lights, being a follow spot operator to helping with the lightboard or the sound system. It was truly about as cool as can be, because remember I was a rock and roll fan maybe a fanatic. I got to see all these great acts right in front of me and I was getting paid to do it. Life could not be better. I did the same thing for sports. I got to walk onto the field where the Cardinals played and mingle with the players. I had some amazing experiences with them and got to meet celebrities such as Jack Buck and Dan Kelly—heroes of my generation. As far as the bands went, I got to see and work for the likes of Heart, Led Zeppelin, Uriah Heep, Van Halen, and yes, even KISS! Working with these bands and seeing what was going on told me I wanted to be on the road doing this for a living. Well, at least for now. You may recall I had a MENSA mentality which meant I like to do 1,000 things at once. So while I would have a great time doing a concert, my mind would shift to thinking, I want to do camera for a hockey game, or be an assistant director for a Steamer soccer game. I just wanted to immerse myself in work. I advise any young person getting into any industry to immerse themselves in the industry and ask the question, "Is there anything I can do to help you?"

This was when my love of the business and my passion for music came together. I became a stagehand with the local stagehand union doing load-ins and load-outs for concerts. I was a roadie. It was during this period I got to meet my other musical heroes: the guys from the Canadian rock band Rush. What a thrill. I got to meet all the guys and even got invited to hit the road with their crew for a while. It was an exciting time to be sure. I learned the difference between wearing jeans and cool boots, throwing a guitar around your neck, and what music theory and performance excellence was really all about. Rush was the bomb live. Precise. Powerful. Passionate. It was an entirely different level of excellence all around.

After my brief stint on the road I was back home in St. Louis with my intense desire to be involved in theater still burning brightly. I would do anything I could to be involved in the theater industry. I studied every aspect of theater production and stagecraft. That's when I got involved with the American Theater in St. Louis. It was a classic 1,500-seat old world theater built by Louis A. Cella, a prominent St. Louis real estate man. It had opened in 1907 as a unit of the William Morris Advanced Vaudeville circuit. When vaudeville began to fade across the country, the American Theatre began to host traveling shows from New York and Chicago. For the next 35 years, the American Theatre played host to a wide variety of stage performers such as Ethel Barrymore, W.C. Fields, Will Rogers, Tallulah Bankhead, and Helen Hayes.

Yet its days at that old Market Street location were numbered. Like Joni Mitchell once sang in her anthemic song "Big Yellow Taxi," they paved paradise and put up a parking lot. After a brief period at the old Shubert Theater on Grand Avenue, the American Theater moved to where it is today, at the location of the former Orpheum Theater on 9th street and St. Charles Avenue.

I share this history because it was intriguing to me, and, something very special happened to me there. I wanted to know everything I could about the history of theater in St. Louis. I found it fascinating and energizing. I had studied a lot of Shakespeare and how they would use candles to light the stage — and later a lamp with no shade to light up the theater. I would go to the theater during off hours and stand on the edge of the stage reciting Shakespeare to a completely empty house. It was enveloped by an eerie glow with me imagining someday it would be a full house who had come to see me. Acting was always on my mind. Maybe, just maybe somebody would come listen to me do it there.

One day while I was there, a show had come to town called "Diversions and Delights," a story about Oscar Wilde. It was a one-man show, and I'll tell you who this is about in a second. But I was there reciting an opening sequence from The Two Gentlemen of Verona. I was doing, "Cease to persuade, my loving Proteus home-keeping youth have ever homely wits." I was doing my thing, when all of a sudden out of the back gallows of the theater, this very deep voice called out, "What are you doing?"

I turned around and there coming into the light from the dark was … Vincent Price. I was floored and I managed to mutter, "Two Gentlemen from Verona."

"It was lovely," he said. In addition to being an iconic actor, many people don't know that Vincent Price is a St. Louis native. I have always been a big fan. He's a great actor known the world over for his iconic roles in horror films, his love of art … and his theater work. And he was the one playing the lead in "Diversions and Delights."

So here I am. Face to face with a legend, having a conversation about Shakespeare. So as we are chatting we move to the edge of the stage and sit down together. We talked for what seemed like hours to me but was probably about 30 minutes. We talked about the arts in general and where he got his start in his various endeavors. At the end of our conversation, he leans in and said quietly but firmly, "Pursue your dream David, always pursue your dream."

I was in the clouds for a year after this. It was a once-in-a-lifetime, amazing experience. I have had the great fortune throughout my life to meet and talk with a lot of people in theater but this one night changed me forever. In moments like these there are no politics. It's all about the craft, perfecting your talents and achieving your artistic goals. Great actors all seem to have one recurring trait: trust. You have to let go completely and expose yourself emotionally. The next time you watch an award show like the Oscars listen to what the actors always say about working with each other. When they give the highest of praise: they talk of how the other actors they work with were so sharing of themselves with them. I have tried to bring that level of being open and sharing of myself into my industry which we'll talk about later. When I was coaching hockey, and getting to learn from some of the great coaches in the NHL because of my work interviewing them for Bud sports, they would use phrases like, "OK, boys, you gotta keep it and leave it all on the ice." What they were saying is in whatever you do, you have to give all of yourself to be successful and to garner the respect of the people around you.

I have never let go of that feeling. I always trust people first and ask questions later. Many people cannot do that. It's not how they were raised. Time has helped me to be somewhat more cautious about this and simply be myself, open and upfront with people in my life. But not everybody is ready for that. It just doesn't resonate with everyone which I find terribly unfortunate. I have always enjoyed conversation and engaging with others full on. I've always loved telling stories, my stories, in hopes of hearing more about theirs. For a long time I was disappointed when folks didn't seem to appreciate that direct, honest approach. It helped with the extreme anxiety I mentioned before. I did understand however when my therapists said, "David, not everybody is like you." I got it. But it really kind of didn't matter to me. I have always believed in getting to the heart of the matter, and when you do that things can get a little bit easier. Life can get a little bit better. Ultimately, this became a guiding force and integral part of my approach to directing and coaching others. I do it now in my day-to-day interactions with clients who have just about everything on the line and are scared to death to present in front of people, whether it's live or on a video conference call.

So that is how I got the confidence — and the idea — to start a video production company which would prove to be a major turning point in my life. More about that in Chapter 5.

CHAPTER 5

"Hollywood Nights. In A Volkswagen."

Los Angeles is a very unforgiving place if you're looking to realize your dreams of making it as an actor. But like thousands of starry-eyed young people, I headed west from St. Louis to LA in the spring of 1981 right after graduating from UMSL. I had a big fire burning in my belly and I was bound and determined to make this thing work. I was experienced and legit because of my college theater acting accolades and felt ready to hit the road. I was Hollywood bound.

I had a plane ticket, a small bag, and not a lot of cash. I think it was like $250. When I arrived, I had enough cash for a few meals and a couple nights in a hotel. I can't remember what hotel. After a few days, I looked up a guy who had been a partner in my Dad's dental practice. He had left St. Louis a year or so before to move to L.A. for another opportunity. His name was Dr. Gil Unatin. He was a pretty hip, cool kind of guy. We met in Long Beach where he lived, caught up and then something amazing happened — he gave me a Volkswagen Beetle to use. I was floored at his generosity — another thing I believe in strongly and which runs throughout the book.

The VW Beetle became my home; I lived in that bug the whole time I was there. A grand total of about six miserable months. I had a terrible run as an actor. Still, I was undeterred.

Needing to find a quick way to make some cash, I decided to use Dr. Unatin's connections to hook me up with people who wanted racquetball lessons. I had been a competitive racquetball player and I thought this might be a way to earn some money as I ventured off to my auditions. I began to teach racquetball in the health club in the bottom of the ABC Entertainment building near the Shubert Theater, which afforded me access to the club's facilities. I did it for a while to buy food and gas. I was also able to take showers in the club locker rooms. Big bonus.

During the first couple of months, I split my time teaching at the club and hanging around with other "actors." Auditions can be ruthless, and the rejection soul crushing. I had a headshot stapled to a paper with, my accomplishments. It wasn't much but it was all I had. Then one day in Long Beach I met a guy who was the best friend of Dr. Unatin. His name was Dennis Hackin, the producer of Clint Eastwood's film "Bronco Billy." He invited me to come see him and a couple days later I went to his office. Now, I only had one suit and it was a Johnny Carson line suit. A brownish looking thing, just a piece-of-shit looking suit. Standing in his office in front of his desk, I was waiting quite anxiously as he was reading my resume while looking several times at my headshot. With a rather heavy sigh, he looked up at me and said matter-of-factly, "You realize there's a thousand people who look like you, and you know you're not that special, right?" I kept saying I was a great actor and he kept saying, "There are thousands of great actors out here." I just couldn't win.

I had been on several auditions already. One time I had an audition where they asked me to slip my picture under the door, I heard people inside laughing. I knocked on the door and went inside and said, "Well, what do you think?" I wasn't prepared for their answer: they tore up my picture in front of me and threw it at me. That was just super. I didn't last long. I was done. The dream was over. I wasn't going to be a Hollywood actor — great or otherwise. But I did have one last glitter of hope of success in Hollywood. Later while talking with Dennis, he remarked, "In looking at your resume, I see you directed a lot." That intrigued him and he said, "Have you ever thought about doing that? Because *that* I can get you into." This piqued my interest and I said, "Sure!" The problem was I didn't have a union card so I couldn't get a real gig as a director. It's kind of a Catch-22 thing.

A few days later, Dennis called and told me to meet him at Columbia Pictures Television. Once there, I was directed to the lot where the TV series Matt Houston was filmed. Lee Horsley was the lead actor who played Matt Houston. So there I was with another director, directing, but I was doing it for free, because I had directed theater but never a motion picture, and I was learning on the fly. One day this guy came in — he was a representative of the Director's Guild. Because this was a union shoot, he said, "You have to get the fuck off this set." As I was leaving, I was thinking, "What else could possibly go wrong?" I was very dejected.

I went back to my car and I had $60 to my name. I was running low. But at the Shubert Theater next to where the racquetball club was, there was a show called "Sophisticated Ladies" which was based on the music of Duke Ellington, and starred Gregory Hines. I had been planning to go home because I just couldn't survive in LA, but I decided "what the hell" and bought a $30 ticket to the show. It was one of the most amazing shows I ever saw. After the show I met up with a friend of mine who was also down in the dumps. We decided to go to a cognac bar for one last hurrah. I had enough money to get to the airport after I dropped off Gil's Volkswagen so we bellied up to the bar. I had ten bucks left. We were gonna have a drink, say goodbye to LA and, "Fuck this place." I was pretty pissed off.

Sitting at the bar, and I asked the bartender, "What's the cheapest thing you've got here that we can afford for ten bucks?" He brought out some crap that was like battery acid. But across the table was uber-fucking Jew, a balding guy in his 50s with an open shirt, all the necklaces one could handle, and an attractive woman sitting next to him. Obviously, a Hollywood producer. So we're watching this guy and checking out how the good life is. He shouts out to the bartender something like, "Harry, get my baby some of the expensive cognac shit." I remember it was like $100 a shot. Now if you're a cognac drinker, you let it sit and you sniff it and go through all the motions, doing everything except making love to it. But this bimbo just slams it down her throat and the whole bar gasps in horror. Producer guy yells over to the bartender, "Get her another one." We were thinking, "Shit, that's more money than we make in a couple of months. We shook our heads and left. I dropped off my friend and the car, then went to the airport and flew home.

So now I am back in St. Louis and still trying to figure it all out. I didn't know what to do, so I started acting in local theater productions.

As I mentioned, by the time I graduated from the University of Missouri in St. Louis, I had amassed a lot of stage hours in plays in a wide variety of roles. I had what I thought was a prolific resume in both equity and non-equity productions. By equity I mean The Actors' Equity Association, often referred to as Actors' Equity or simply Equity for short. Equity was an American labor union representing actors in the world of live theatrical performance. To join Equity, you have to complete a membership application and pay the required initiation fee and ongoing Basic dues and Working dues. I was legit in this world. I was with the Kirkwood Theater Guild where I did "A Streetcar Named Desire" and I played Alan Strang in "Equus" which was wild. A lot of deep-seated psychological stuff going on with that role. One of my favorite roles was with the St. Louis City Players where I did "Elephant Man" and played the main character Joseph Merrick, the real Elephant Man; which is a horrible name. He was gravely physically deformed. I remember having had the absolute privilege of seeing David Bowie in a mind-blowing performance in that role in Chicago. It's a part very much for dancers because of the physical demands to make it come across on the theater stage. And boy did David Bowie master all of that. He made the character come alive. No prosthetics, no makeup beyond the norm. It was all body mechanics, facial tics, and voice control. As he is being described by the narrator, he begins to transform and contort his body and his voice to create the illusion of the Elephant Man. Just a brilliant performance because you have to keep that up for the entire two hours you are on stage. For me, probably my favorite performance was in "The Ascent of F6" by W.H. Auden, in which I committed suicide on stage. Ironically, I jumped off a mountain which is kind of interesting because I later became a mountain climber and narrowly missed getting killed in an avalanche.

In addition to my theatrical performances, I had also done several TV commercials and was repped by a local talent agency called Talent Plus.

About the time I got a part as an extra in the Kurt Russell film "Escape From New York." I don't think it was widely known, but that movie was filmed almost entirely in St. Louis with some of the scenes also shot in Los Angeles. Another interesting note is the "Manhattan" skylines in the film were mostly all mattes. A matte is a composite of multiple images to create a new image or backdrop. The opening scene of the film showed Manhattan very dark at night. The island had become a prison for the underbelly of society. All the riffraff and criminals were taken there. It was regarded, like Alcatraz in San Francisco, as inescapable. In the opening scene, a raft of prisoners attempting to escape was destroyed. But it wasn't the East or Hudson rivers of Manhattan they were on, but rather an inlet off the coast of Long Beach, California. Ahh, the magic of moviemaking.

At the time of filming, I was part of an acting troupe in St. Louis called The City Players. One day we heard through the grapevine something big was coming in St. Louis. We learned it was going to be an action film starring Kurt Russell. It was a big deal. We were all pumped when we heard from our talent rep they were going to be doing auditions for bit players and extras. In fact, the local paper had an ad about it in the classified section — looking for "crazies, lunatics and psychos." Perfect. The ad said something like, "If you're a guy, don't shave that day. The rougher you look the better. If you're a woman, the sleazier the better." If you've seen the film, you know what I mean.

You probably couldn't get away with that kind of language or description today, but back then you could. So a bunch of us went to the offices of Talent Plus in Clayton, Missouri, the suburb I had grown up in, to see if we could get an audition.

When we showed up, there was this *really* long line wrapping completely around the area about ten people thick. Everybody and their sister had come down for this thing. There were all kinds of people there. Bikers, crazy people, and drugs. You name it. Everybody was auditioning. After a long wait, we finally got to the audition room. They were bringing ten people in at a time. The casting team sat behind a couple of card tables and as we all approached, they just went "Yes, you'll do, no, no, no". That was pretty much how it went. Now I was Mr. Pretty Boy at the time. I was completely shaven and was a stark contrast to this motley crew. But I got a "yes". The long story is I had about two seconds on screen as an extra where I was the second guy that climbs out of a sewer. That was it. But it was a pretty cool experience for a very young man.

My dad was getting to the point where he said I really had to get a "real" job because he wanted me to stop living at home and make my way into the real world. That's when my life took yet another big turn.

CHAPTER 6

"Lights. Camera. Action."

S ometimes you just have to speak up.

I cannot stress enough how important it is to speak your mind in your profession. To be determined and with purpose. Not to be great. But to be just what you can to the best of your potential. It can mean the difference between moving from bad to good and good to great. Don't ever be bashful if you know what the hell you are talking about. I'll explain more here shortly how that can change a project. And, in my case, changed the direction of my career yet again.

When I took film editing in college, I learned all the old school, manual methods of quite literally cutting apart and piecing together pieces of tape frame by frame. It was painstaking, often frustratingly long and mind-numbingly detailed work. But I learned all about the craft of moviemaking in great detail. And it all was about to pay off, which brings me to Harold Ramis, the famous actor from "Ghostbusters" and "Animal House" fame. It turns out he was the first cousin of my second wife so I kind of inherited him and I got to meet him at a few family functions. He was a really cool, nice guy. He went to Washington University in

St. Louis and his hi-jinks there were the basis for the screenplay he wrote for "Animal House."

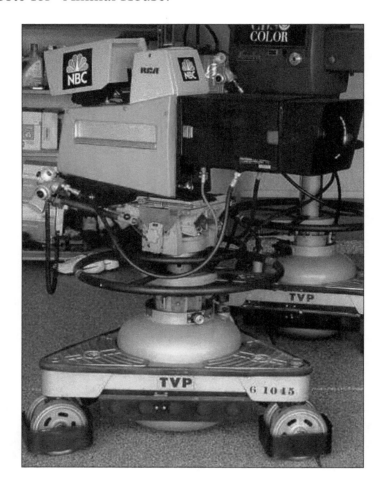

Around this time my dad, who was pretty keen to get me a real job, got me an interview at the local PBS affiliate KETC, Channel 9, which was located near the frat house that Harold Ramis belonged to. It is kind of a weird coincidence how this set my career in motion. I met with this PBS producer who said he could get me in as a cameraman since I had studied filmmaking in college. He put me in the studio as a camera operator for the PBS pledge drives they did on TV. Now I also had my union card for acting, so in addition to doing the camera work, I also got to be in front of the camera doing the dollar tallies for the drives. It was called the Quickie Board so I got to do some funny improv stuff (at least I thought it was funny at the time). One day during a pledge drive, I made a joke on air about Zsa Gabor. You may recall she was a world-famous Hungarian-American actress and socialite. She had two sisters who also were actresses, Eva and Magda Gabor. Zsa Gabor initially started her stage career in Vienna and was crowned Miss Hungary in 1936. She emigrated from Hungary to the United States in 1941 and the rest is history. Well, my mom called me up after that and said "I bet Zsa is going to call you to talk to you about that, David!" It turns out they were distant cousins. My Dad's middle name is actually Gabor. So that was kind of crazy. And no, I never did hear from Zsa.

I continued to do various gigs at the PBS station. We used huge old RCA cameras which were on large pedestals with wheels and hydraulics so they could move up and down easily. By today's standards, of course, they were behemoths and rather unwieldy, but they were pretty cool at the time. I would constantly practice zooming in and zooming out. Moving the camera across the floor, panning. All the moves you need to be good at your craft. It's not as easy as it may look. There's a lot going on. The lighting has to be right, the lenses have to be clean, the cameras have to stay cool. Just a lot of things to be aware of as you are filming. You also have to know how the cameras work and how to take care of them. In fact the old three tube cameras were very sensitive. They had these super thick 56-pin cables and if you bent just one pin even a little bit, you would screw up the signal, so you had to be very careful. We also had these three-tube cameras with the red, green and blue tubes which burn out easily just by having too much light directly on them. In fact, I burned out one of those cameras during an outdoor shoot because I didn't factor in the heat of the sun on the cameras. You could actually fix those tubes by taking the burned tube out, putting it in a plastic locking baggie and storing it in the freezer for two days. It makes putting a wet cell phone in rice these days look easy.

While working at PBS I was able to get my IBEW union card which was a big deal for me to get gigs and get good at filming live events. I was an outsider but was meeting more and more people in the industry. I honed my skills doing Cardinal Baseball games at Busch Stadium. You start out in Center Field which is the easiest camera to operate because it doesn't require much movement. Then you would graduate to low first base, high first base and the home plate camera which was the "hero" camera because it captured everything from pitches to infield plays to home runs. I would practice filming the guys shagging balls, so I got really good technically at all of those skills — and became an accomplished camera operator. I also was doing St. Louis Blues hockey games and having a blast. The next stop was to work in the remote trucks doing replays where I would learn the ropes of being an editor. I was soaking it all in and moving up the ranks pretty quickly.

I like to say I became a real "vidiot" because I was so intensely into everything about camera operations and film editing. I loved the technology. I was also working as a stagehand and would help load in and load out and operate follow spotlights for concerts. I was doing everything you can imagine to immerse myself in all areas of producing and recording live events. Eventually I got work at ABC, NBC, CBS and even Channel 30, the independent channel in St. Louis. I got to do repair work. I remember once climbing a 1,200-foot broadcast tower out in the middle of nowhere to change the light bulb. Just for reference, that is twice the height of the famous St. Louis Arch. I am here to tell you those things mostly sway in the wind. But I was young and thought it all was pretty cool, heady stuff. I'd never do that now of course, but youth can make you feel invincible. By this time I had all my union cards to work behind and in front of the camera. I moved from being behind the camera to the editing suite.

Here's where speaking up comes in. For a long time, editing was high on my list of goals as I had done some editing in high school and college and liked being able to help tell stories through the magic of editing. I really learned my craft on the job as a union editor in St. Louis. One day I got this gig to work on a documentary at PBS in St. Louis about Twyla Tharpe, the world-famous dancer and dance instructor. Now remember, I had formally studied dance, and not only knew her work well but had danced to her routines, so I was excited to work as a union editor on the gig.

We were in the studio doing post-production on the film and I was working with a producer (let's call him Craig) who turned out to be a real asshole. A prima donna bar none. As the morning progressed, Craig was making what I thought were some questionable editing decisions. I knew the routines and I knew every frame of the film we were working with, so I made a suggestion. He ignored me. We kept going and I made another couple of suggestions. Well, evidently, he didn't want to hear any more from me, the lowly editor. He looked at me and literally shouted, "Look, your job is to listen to me, push the fucking buttons and do what I want you to do. If I want your opinion, I will ask you for it."

Being the good union do-bee I was, I shrugged it off, kept my mouth shut, and kept editing. Well, after about the fourth time hearing Craig berate me, the executive producer and the director asked Craig to step outside. After the door closed, I heard a lot of yelling. A lot of loud screaming really. I just sat there minding my own little union editor business. This went on for a few minutes.

After the screaming had subsided, executive producer and director came back into the edit suite and they said, "Hey, we really liked your ideas. How would you feel about finishing up the show? We'll even give you a production and direction credit."

Now you can imagine the utter joy I felt at that moment. The asshole was out and I, the good do bee union editor, was now in complete control of the film. I said okay and went back to work but not before I said, "I DO think we need to reshoot some scenes." Which they gave me the green light to do. I was thrilled.

So the documentary got edited, produced, and aired on PBS. Evidently, it was a success, but little did I know how much of a success. One day several months later I was working away on another project shooting some scenes and I got a message through my headset. I was told that something was waiting for me up in the conference room on the second floor. I hustled up and entered the room and there were all the people I had worked with on the documentary.

As I entered the room, they all smiled and said, "Hey man, how are you doing?" Perplexed, I stammered, "Uh fine. What's up?" One of the producers said, "Well, you didn't know this, but we loved the documentary so much that we entered it into the regional Emmy Award competition."

"Really?" I said not understanding where any of this was going.

"Yeah, and you won't believe this." They pointed to a table with a black cloth draped over something. I didn't know what. Then they lifted up the black velvet cloth and there was an Emmy Award with my name on it. I froze for a second and thought to myself, "Holy crap, is this for real?" I had won the regional Emmy for Best Director. I was completely flabbergasted. Talk about proud. I was on cloud nine.

After I left PBS, I worked briefly shooting and editing for a company called AVP Communications, which stood for Associated

Visual Productions. We would shoot restaurant commercials on the Hill in St. Louis where all the Italian restaurants are. They would play on channel 3 in the hotel TV systems. Pretty dull stuff, but during the course of this brief period, we met a lot of what we later learned were Mafia members. It was all rather weird.

I decided I needed to do something drastically different, and it was around this time I decided to start my own company "Lights. Camera. Action." I loved the name from watching an interview with Alfred Hitchcock. He was talking about the difference between shock and suspense. He said, "At the end of the day it really is no different than lights, camera, action." I loved that, did some digging, and found out the name was available — so that's what I named the company. My interest had turned to where the money was, which was corporate video.

I took on various projects and it was a lot of fun. After a year or so I recall being asked, "How did you get in this business?" I immediately said you have to get immersed in the industry. If you have to carry a cable, carry the damned cable. Because you will be on set. You're doing something. You are involved. So just do it. Go do anything you can. I remember one time when I was a cable runner, I got into trouble with one of the union guys. I was working with what they called "horse cock" cables because they were really thick. Not kidding, that's what they were called. And they weighed a ton. They were made mostly of copper and came in these huge 50-foot runs. There was this big, tough union guy who looked like a longshoreman, who had this thick Chicago accent and would always use this phrase, "Know what I'm sayin'?" I remember thinking, "Fuck, yes. I know what you're saying," and would roll my eyes. He told me to go over and dress stack these cables, which I did. Dress stacking means you have to roll up the cable and tie it off with a piece of rope. Young and energetic I finished the task rather quickly. But this guy looked at me and said, "What the fuck are you doin'? You're makin' us all look bad here. Go undo it and do it a lot slower. We're getting' paid by the hour here and I gotta get a lunch in."

It was then I knew I wanted something more. I really needed to be my own boss. Ironically, I ended up hiring a lot of those same union guys when I started "Lights. Camera. Action." because most of them were really good at their jobs. I worked for a few years doing corporate stuff and the occasional agency gig. Agencies would call up looking to hire production companies. Typically, I would go in and meet with agency's Creative Director and give them my pitch. Incidentally, the tag line for my company was, "We're Almost Always On Time" which I thought was funny. I am a smart-ass you know. We had created a promotional video we shot in black and white. It showed a close-up of a clock waking me up and me scrambling around the house trying to get to a gig. People seemed to really like the self-deprecating humor of it. I felt strongly about this approach because we were actually very structured, and I was very demanding that my crews to be on time, and to do the shoots as efficiently and professionally as possible.

I remember one day getting a call from a small, boutique agency in St. Louis from a guy named Steve Penn. He helped me put this book together and has been a dear friend for 30 years. Steve had just got a job as the Creative Director at this agency and one of their big clients was a national sports magazine called "The

Sporting News" — which got its start in St. Louis. The agency he worked for did their subscription marketing and they were looking to do a direct response TV commercial for them. Now Steve was an ex-newspaper reporter turned ad guy, but he also had a minor in film, and had written and produced a national TV commercial for Mutual of Omaha which featured a partnership with Michael Wayne, John Wayne's son, and starred his other son Patrick Wayne. The spot ran for about three years I think, and Steve was anxious to get back to doing TV spots. He pitched me the opportunity and wanted to know if I was interested, which of course sounded great to me. So, being diligent, I worked up a treatment on a brief storyboard. It featured a lot of stock sports action footage playing inside the logo of the magazine as it came into focus from small letter to full screen. He loved it. Unfortunately, the magazine had changed its mind about doing TV and stuck with print and direct mail so that gig fell through. Steve went on to another agency a few months after that.

Meanwhile, I kept on trucking. I did a few more shoots but it was a tough go. Up and down. It had been down for a while when one day I got a call from a hospital that was opening a birthing center in Texas. I got the gig and sent a crew down to Texas to handle the shoot. I was planning to meet them there the next day or so. At the time, I was visiting my mom in Florida. that's when my world just fell apart. I got a call saying the Texas shoot had been cancelled. I freaked out. My bank account was low already and I was going to have to pay for the crew down in Texas. I began to panic. Really panic. My anxiety gripped me so tightly I didn't know what to do. But my mom, being the ever calm and wise spirit she was, said, "Don't worry about this. Let's go drive up to the Cape." I had been a huge fan of NASA and space travel and all that particular world was about. The Cape was Cape Canaveral. She wanted to take me to see the rockets there. It made me feel a bit at ease. That's when I got the call from my friend Steve. He had a project for me. I can't tell you how much it changed my life at that point. The gig paid $25,000 which was a lot of money. I was thrilled.

That job proved to come with its own little adventure which literally nearly scared me to death. Steve's new agency had a long-time client called Silgan Plastics, one of the world's largest plastic bottle manufacturers. They had locations all over the country and in Canada. They were looking to do a corporate video that showed the process of making bottles from start to finish. Our job was to fly to their plant in Ligonier, Indiana and spend three days shooting in their plant to show how it all worked; the safety measures they had in place at the plant, and why their process was so innovative and valuable to their clients. Steve and I worked up a creative treatment, I hired a crew, and Silgan Plastics arranged to fly us all to Ft. Wayne, Indiana for the shoot on their private plane. We would drive 40 miles to their location in a van packed with gear. It was a beautiful day when we arrived at the airport. We were laughing and making jokes about plastics as we loaded our gear into the small turbo prop jet and took off. Now the flight is about three hours or so and the first half was uneventful. Later as we looked out the windows of the plane, we noticed the weather was changing rapidly. It got very dark, very quickly. We saw lightning flashing all around us. The plane began to shake violently and pitch from side to side. Stuff was flying out of compartments all over the plane. We looked at each other and thought we were going to die in the next few moments. Then, suddenly, it all stopped. The plane leveled off and the sky cleared. We were alive. When the plane landed, we all got out and I remember kneeling down and kissing the tarmac at the airport. It was the craziest plane ride of my life to this very day — I have been on a few. We wrapped up the gig, which went beautifully, and returned to the airport. When

I got on the plane, I noticed it was the same pilot. I poked my head through curtains to the cockpit and said, "Please tell me this flight is going to be better." The pilot looked at me and said, "Oh, yeah, you're the guys who were on that flight a few days ago when we went through the storm. That was some fun, huh?"

Yeah. That was fun.

CHAPTER 7

"Scaling New Heights"

S ometimes you have to climb a mountain. Just to prove you can. Growing up in the cultural sphere and influence of Eastern European parents, two things were always impressed upon me from a very young age: Education and sports. I was really good at one of those.

I have covered my struggles in school with grades and bullying earlier in this book. But here I want to take a look back at what I call the "adventurous me." I truly believe the success I have had in my career flows from the competitive spirit instilled in me at an early age, and a natural instinct in all that I have done as an adult. It's one of the reasons I do so much research on my business competition and why I counsel my clients about understanding how they can best position themselves to win lucrative government contracts. You have to be bold. You have to have the courage to take steps you have never taken before. You have to have faith in yourself, your business, and your objectives. Set your goals high and reach as high and far as you can. Even higher than you ever knew you could.

For me, sports were an intrinsic part of my life beginning at the age of just four. It started with little things like going to the local outdoor ice-skating rink in Shaw Park in Clayton, Missouri. By the time I was five, I was playing hockey in what they called a Mini Mite league. We had all this equipment piled onto our tiny little frames. It could get surprisingly cold in the winter in St. Louis, especially for little kids. It was common then to put plastic bags on our feet and a couple pair of socks then our skates. We were bundled up damned near airtight. After we were done skating, we all headed straight to the fire pit at the end of the rink and then back out on the ice. We didn't care about the cold really. We were four and five years old. It was just plain fun. This was the beginning of my life-long love of skating ... and my passion for hockey.

A few years later as I was getting better and better at skating, we learned St. Louis was getting a hockey team in the NHL expansion of 1967. They were called the St. Louis Blues, which was the name of a song by famous bluesman W.C. Handy. It was a big deal. Everybody went nuts that we were getting a hockey team. And boy were they good. They won their division and went on to the Stanley Cup finals in 1967, 1968 and 1969. Being a Blues fan would become a big deal for me. I collected player cards, uniforms, sticks, skates ... anything with the Blues logo on it. I went on to play in hockey leagues starting with the Mini Mites league. I played up through high school and college either in leagues or in pick-up games with friends. One memory I have is as a kid skating regularly with Blues defenseman Jean-Guy Talbot whose son was on my team. What a thrill to skate with and be coached by a world-famous defenseman who would later become the Blues head coach in 1972. Very cool for a little kid. Years later I would get to hang out with the team and skate with them in the Blues Alumni League.

My other passion at a young age in sports was tennis. I would go out and play tennis with my dad for hours on end — and got very good at it. He had a membership at a local tennis club, and we played doubles a lot. It was a lot of fun. I joined a league and was very competitive. In fact when I was 15, I won the Dwight Davis National Junior Championship. I loved tennis but my coach Russ Dipold was a power player and believed in intimidating his opponents. He taught me to just keep crushing the ball the same way he did — super aggressively. He would load up a shopping cart full of balls, place small linoleum tiles in various spots on the other side of the net, and feed me ball after ball after ball, yelling at me to "hit the ball" at a particular tile — a whole shopping cart full of them. Then move to the next tile and do the same. We would do this for hours at a time several days a week until I couldn't hit anymore. I got burned out and began to feel this just wasn't my style. I wasn't a naturally aggressive person. It didn't work for me because I would commit too many errors during matches just wailing on the ball. I wanted a more controlled, thoughtful approach to the game. I preferred the Bjorn Borg style of playing where you wore your opponent down methodically by keeping the ball in play and letting the other guy make the mistakes. After a while I just kind of lost interest in tennis and had become fascinated with racquetball. I would still play doubles with my parents and friends but the fire to play competitively was gone and racquetball took center stage as my sport of choice. If you know anything about tennis and racquetball, you realize they are very different in terms of the physical skills required to be good at them. I loved every aspect of racquetball and I had soon mastered the sport pretty well, too. If I had stuck with tennis, who knows what I might have achieved. But racquetball was calling. I played it for years, winning tournaments and eventually teaching as a pro at the local club. It was good for my ego and kept my anxiety at bay.

Sports was a gateway to other physical pursuits in my life. I loved the adrenalin rush of doing something that pushed my body and my mind to their limits. I enjoyed the challenge of working toward a goal and achieving it. It's a trait which would hold me in good stead in my career; and the passionate pursuit of a wide range of new and exciting adventures in life, such as spelunking. If you're not familiar with the term, spelunking, also called caving, is a recreational pastime where you explore wild cave systems, often deep underground.

When I was 17, I became involved in spelunking quite by accident. My childhood buddy Louis and I would take off on crazy trips, often not knowing where we were going or why until we were on the road. Once we travelled to Evansville, Indiana to track down this girl I was madly in love with. She was in a band that had played in St. Louis. I knew where she lived so we just took off. We headed to Evansville, but never found this gal. We had a couple days to kill, so we took off for Kentucky for no particular reason and stayed in a hotel about two hours south of Evansville. In the lobby of the hotel there was a rack with maps and brochures of things to do in the area. One of them was a brochure about spelunking at the famous Mammoth Cave National Park. Now THIS sounded interesting. I had been to Meramec Caverns in Missouri, so I thought, "Sure why not?" Well, Meramec Caverns is like a nice little stroll through a natural museum. But spelunking at Mammoth Caves? We would learn it was an entirely different activity. Some spelunking trips can last for several days. We signed up for an eight-hour expedition and had no idea what to expect. On the day of the trip we arrived and there were eight of us in the group led by a medical student who did expeditions part time. Now you have to remember Mammoth Cave is one of the largest cave systems in the world, second only to Son Doong Cave in Vietnam.

We learned some interesting things on this expedition, one of which is I did not truly understand the concept of darkness until I went on this expedition — but I was about to learn. About halfway through our spelunk we arrived at this open area and our guide told us to shut off our helmet lights. So everybody turned off their lights. It was pitch black. It's one thing to close your eyes in the darkness of your house or outside at night. You still actually get light through your eyelids. But being a couple hundred feet underground in a cave is an entirely different level of complete and utter darkness. It's a very unnerving experience. It's one thing to close your eyes but when you have your eyes wide open and you can't even see your hand when you wave it front of your face, that's crazy dark. Really spooky.

Once we turned our lights back on, we continued to explore, seeing all kinds of wild sights like cave crickets. These are insects with long antennae and eyes attached to the end so they can see in their environment. Another part of the cave was called the Crystal Palace which is composed of extremely thin rock formations. When I say thin, I mean like the thickness of a string of hair thin. If you moved near them the motion of the air from your movements would cause them to shatter and crackle to the floor. It takes thousands of years for them to slowly form, and it was the most gorgeous thing I had ever seen. Simply stunning. As we continued on this particular little jaunt, we did this thing called a Canyon Walk where we had to straddle a small open corridor over a stream about 100 feet below with a wall on one side and a very, very narrow ledge a few inches wide on the other. There were no ropes or ladders, you just kind of shuffle your way through. As I was doing this, I kept thinking *"I hope I don't die. I hope I don't die."*

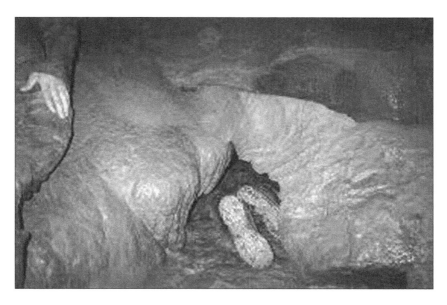

After we navigated the passage, we entered another open area and our guide told us one of the things we had to do on this little jaunt through Mammoth Cave was crawl our way through what was called The Mole Hole. A passage that extends 15 feet into another area of the cave. It's on a 20% incline and it's only about 48 inches in diameter. Basically you're in an extended coffin-like tube of solid rock. If your head is not in the right place, it's easy to freak out. Our guide went first — I watched him crawl through until his legs disappeared. I peered into the hole and could faintly make out that he was on the other side. *That's not so bad, I thought"*. When it was my turn, I turned to Louis who was next and said. "Hey buddy, when I start going through this hole, do me a favor and give me a push on my feet when I say 'push', so I have a little more leverage."

Now, Louis loved to pull pranks and mess with me all the time. But what came next was not really funny at the time. I mean I already was getting anxious. As I wriggled into the hole, I yelled "Push!" and what did Louis do? You guessed it: he pulled my legs back a bit and I went into full-blown a panic attack right then and there. I was scared to death. I yelled at him to let go, but he just laughed. I asked the guide to grab my hand and pull me through but he said, "Nope. You have to do it on your own." After I screamed at Louis again, he let go and I made it through the Mole Hole. I wanted to kill Louis. We laugh about it today but boy did it freak me out at the time. Still it was an amazing experience. As we were emerging from our climb into the sunlight at the end of the expedition I remember looking down at my clothes, then we all kind of looked at each other. We were covered head to toe in mud, slime and grime. I'm sure it looked like we had been trapped in a mine for a month. The area where we exited was a public tour stop and people all around were looking at us and gasping as they walked past. I thought, *"They must think we are real bad-asses."* It was a cool feeling and made the whole experience all the more worth it. This was my one and only experience caving, but I'll never forget it.

Probably the most exciting, dangerous, challenging, and physically exhausting thing I have ever done is mountain climbing. I never had the desire to do it. I had never even thought about it. But the bug bit me on a trip to Washington state when I tried to rekindle a relationship with my first wife Carolyn. This was around 1988. We both had missed each other and thought we should give our marriage one more attempt. She had secured a work gig in Seattle and invited me out to meet and stay with her for a few days. I would have some time to myself while she worked.

One of the things you notice when you're in Seattle on a clear day is you can see Mt. Rainier in the distance. It's an incredibly impressive sight. The day after I arrived, Carolyn went to work, and I decided to take a drive. I grabbed a map and decided to head out to get a better look at Mt. Rainier. As I drove down the highway towards this impressive glacial behemoth it got bigger and bigger by the mile. I had no idea it was so huge and was overwhelmed not only by its size but its majesty and beauty. As you wind your way up the road, every turn reveals something more spectacular than the last. The white glacial slopes set against the gorgeous azure sky was a visual treat. I had never seen anything like it.

After a couple of hours, I returned back and had dinner with Carolyn. As we ate, I couldn't contain my excitement and told her all about the drive. She suggested we should both go the next day because she had time off. So that's what we did. The drive to the main area at the foot of the mountain takes about three and a half hours.

At the base of the mountain at about 5,000 feet there's a gorgeous lodge called the Paradise Inn. It's one of the largest inns of its type in the world and it's stunning in its elegant design and commanding presence — with Mt. Rainier looming large behind it. The lobby is amazing and there is a huge dining hall so we decided to have lunch there. After we ate, we were walking around the grounds and saw these guys walking in these big, heavy-looking boots with spikes on the bottom. They had pickaxes and huge backpacks, with faces that looked like raccoons — really dark, tanned faces and whites all around their eyes.

As Carolyn and I stood there looking up at the mountain, this big, rugged-looking, long-haired guy comes up to us and says in a Valley Girl-type voice "Pretty bitchin', eh?" We were like, "Yeah, this is so amazing." He said, "You should climb up there, man." Of course, knowing nothing about mountain climbing, I said, "People go up there?" He looked at me and said, "Oh, yeah man, it's a great climb. You camp up there. You can do the climb up and back in two days."

I must have had a dumb look on my face, but this actually got me thinking about it. I was intrigued if not a little overwhelmed at the idea and as I stood there thinking and staring up at the mountain, Carolyn said "You could never make it." That was it. The gauntlet had been thrown down and I thought about it during the flight back to St. Louis. Once I got home, I went to the library and started reading about mountain climbing. I visited some sports stores that sold climbing gear and met with some climbers in St. Louis, which admittedly is not the mecca of mountain climbing. That did it. I was sucked in. I was bound and determined to go climb that freaking mountain.

I started training. Now training for this sort of thing is incredibly taxing on your body. One of the things you do is climb stairs. I had done some work with Southwestern Bell, and I got permission to use their stairwell to train in. All 56 floors of it. My first few efforts were ten floors, and I would be done for the day. Just totally spent. This was all in the middle of summer. I started climbing the stairs one at a time with my new glacier boots, bike shorts, a T-shirt and bandana. Then I would add weight until I was climbing the stairs with the equivalent of a full pack you would use to actually climb up a mountain. It was grueling, exhausting work. But I did it. By the time I was ready for my first climb on Rainier, I had been going up and down those stairs with 50 pounds of weights in a backpack. I started off doing one step at a time and then two, then three steps at a time. My legs got immense. I soon would learn climbing stairs is not like climbing on ice. After my training I headed to Seattle again where I signed up for a five-day expedition training seminar.

My lead training guide was a guy named Bob Link who was a big deal in mountain climbing. He was a mountain man's mountain man. He's done it all. He did K2. He did McKinley, he did Everest and more around the world. Several times. He was a legend in the business. He had the tips of his fingers missing from frost bite, and scars on his abdomen from injuries. He was completely dark just like the raccoon guys I had met on my first trip to Seattle. But, he was a really chill guy and made me feel comfortable and safe.

The next day we started training starting with how to pack your backpack. We were given a checklist of items to bring. Now, I'm a classic over-packer, which would provide the guys with a never-ending source of belly laughs. By the time I got done with my checklist, my pack weighed almost 80 pounds and I could hardly even put it on. Now Bobby was the guy who did my pack check. He lifts up my pack and says, "What's this? You don't plan on taking this up there, do you?" He was so calm about it all, but he still made me feel like an idiot. Which, of course, I really was. He opened the pack and asked me why I had five pair of socks. I told him one for each day of the climb. He tossed out four pair and said, "No. Just one pair for all five days." Then he saw my toothbrush and promptly broke off the handle and said, you only need this part bringing the brush up to his teeth with his fingers. Next up were two 35-mm cameras I planned to bring to document the expedition. "Why do you need two cameras?" he asked. "In case one breaks," I replied. At which point, and I kid you not, he smashed the camera to the ground. I was horrified but somehow, I understood. By the time he got done, my pack weighed 35 pounds. Of course, there was the food I was bringing.

I had packed two power bars. He said, "Good luck eating those up there when they're frozen like a brick." I had also packed soap, which he found funny. Yup. No need to clean your body while on this expedition. Just more weight. Once we all had successfully packed a practical pack, we gathered them up and put them all aside.

Next up was our orientation training. The guy who showed up for the orientation was the infamous Pete Whittaker, founder of the outdoor retail chain REI. Pete and his brother were two of the first Americans ever to summit Everest. These guys were big, like 6'5" and ripped. Pete gave an inspiring pep talk which made us all really excited for this amazing adventure we were about to embark on.

We went around the corner carrying our backpacks and there were white bags lying on the ground. We were all told to pick up a bag and put it in our backpacks. This was our food for the trip and each bag weighed 20 pounds. I knew then why I had to get my pack to 35 pounds. The bags were labeled with D1 AM and D1 PM and so on. We didn't know what it meant. I finally figured out it was the day and time of day. Breakfast, lunch and dinner. The secret was NOT to pick up D5 because you would have to carry the damn thing all five days! Or so we thought. The truth was that if you got rid of your food on the first day, you would have the job of carrying the solid human waste from the group because you don't leave that on the mountain. At one point each of us ended up carrying a well-sealed bag of shit during the expedition.

So off we went towards the gleaming glacier that was calling us to conquer it. Our route took us on the more dangerous, exposed side of the mountain. It was hard work. At the end of the day we were beat. I wasn't sure if I could sleep on a mountain, but I managed. It was surreal and I survived the night. The next morning we awoke and there was a storm below us. The only time I had ever seen a storm below me was from the comfort of an airliner 35,000 feet in the sky. This was entirely magical and scary as hell at the same time. We were so close to this storm. We were at 11,000 feet and the storm was at about 8,000. You could feel it. In fact, we could feel a fair amount of rumbling. The ground seemed to be getting unstable and that was unsettling. We set off to reach a scree about two hours up the glacial face from us. A scree is a collection of broken rock fragments and Bob, our guide, had gone ahead to look it over. After a while we saw him walking back towards us. When he got to us, he said, "Look guys, this area is really unstable. Make sure your packs are cinched down tight, don't talk and let's get through this scree area as quickly as we can." We set off for the scree line and once across we planned to head up a steep rocky crevasse to our next camp location. But I never made it.

As we walked, we heard a lot of rumbling. Looking up, we saw a small part of the glacier wall calve off, sending tons of rock and scree our way. We were sitting ducks. Fortunately, most of the debris in this small avalanche fell to the top and right of us, but one large rock about the size of a Volkswagen Beetle came rumbling toward us and passed directly between me and the guy on the rope line behind me. It actually pulled us up off our feet. Just 20 feet to the right or left and one of us would have been crushed. So, the climb was cancelled, and I did not make the summit. But 18 months later I would go back and do it all over again — and make the summit. It was an amazing experience which capped off a chapter in my life I fondly call "The Adventurous Me". I gained an incredible sense of accomplishment.

One thing happened I hadn't counted on, which was the depression that follows accomplishing something so monumental.

I was told it was common, but it hit me hard. While I have fond memories of eventually making it up that mountain both metaphorically and in reality, I still have scary thoughts at night about the avalanche.

But you know what.? I survived. I did it! It was the greatest feeling in the world. Exactly what I inspire my clients to feel.

No matter how high their own personal mountains may be.

CHAPTER 8

"Meanwhile, Back In L.A.: Woody Allen And Hot Dogs In Champagne Glasses."

My return to Los Angeles in 1993 turned out to be both a disaster and a blessing in disguise.

I had been married once, but only for nine months. Several years later I had met and married my second wife. Without going into a lot of detail, she had worked at Monsanto in St. Louis for several years. But one day in the spring of 1993, she came home and told me she had accepted a position as a Human Resources Manager for the submarine division of AlliedSignal in Sylmar, just north of LA. The company, AlliedSignal, was famous for developing the first underwater signaling system for U.S. Navy submarines. Honeywell would buy them out later in 1999.

At that time she earned more than I did and had great benefits, so her job was the number one priority in our household. When she was offered the position, we both eagerly agreed this was a great opportunity. So off we went to LA and found a place to live in Valencia about 20 minutes north of her new company. Things were fine at first, but cracks began to appear in our relationship which would ultimately prove fatal to our marriage.

Soon after we settled into LA, things began to get a bit dicey. My wife kept telling me I needed to get a "real job" and wasn't all that nice about it. As a person already suffering from anxiety, this was not helpful at all. I buckled down and began to look for that "real job." Back in those days, there was no Zip Recruiter or Indeed or Monster boards to easily find jobs online. But my wife's company had a job search firm called Wright and Associates. I connected with them, which proved to be exactly what I needed to not only get a real job but to take the first step in what was ultimately a life-changing career change. They secured an interview for me with Rockwell Aerospace. I impressed the client enough that I was offered a job in their marketing department for a whopping $67,500 a year. Great pay in those days.

I finally had a "real job." And what a job that was: I was put in charge of marketing for the NASA Space Shuttle program, which was a huge shift in my fortunes — and when my career really took off. Things also got interesting in my personal life, meeting some of my-heroes in Hollywood, thanks to my sister Victoria.

Vicky had moved to California a few years earlier and had just met her soon-to-be husband Lloyd Silverman, a producer at Universal Studios in Hollywood. She was a vice president at the prestigious American Film Institute (AFI), and they had become a hot Hollywood couple. I remember one of her friends from her early school years in St. Louis was a gal named Natalie Zimmerman who became an international model at the age of 16. She was stunningly beautiful. She also was married to

Keith Addis, big time movie producer known for his work on Taxi Driver and other hits. She would host huge parties at their Hollywood mansion and that's where I got to meet people like Michael Dorn and some of the actors from Star Trek. I also got to know their best friend Buddy Morra who helped launch and manage the careers of so many household names in the business, including Robin Williams, Billy Crystal, Robert Klein, JoAnn Worley, David Letterman, Martin Mull, Jim Carrey, Marty Short, and Dana Carvey, among others. I have to say Buddy and his wife Carol were the nicest, sweetest people you could ever hope to meet. He was very popular and beloved right up until he passed away in 2019.

They would throw a big Chanukah party every year and I was fortunate to have been on the invitation list for a few of them. I got to meet so many really cool people as a result, including the great comedic actor, Tom Poston. I remember him coming up to me and asking me who I was. I mean I was the schmuck in the room, right? I shyly mentioned I was Victoria's brother. He asked me what I did for a living, and I told him. Well, he was absolutely fascinated by that, which kind of blew me away. He asked me all kinds of questions. Later on I invited him out to see the shuttle and he was just like a little kid. I also got to meet one of my all-time heroes, Milton Berle. I was sitting in the corner on a folding chair eating, and he came up to me with a cigar in his mouth and said, "Who are you here with, kid?" He was in his 80s at the time and married to his third wife, fashion designer Lorna Adams, who was in her 40s. And it's true what they say ... he used to like to brag about being well endowed. It was hilarious. I remember JoAnn Worley and her husband got up an sang a showtune for Buddy and Carol. It was so operatic and over the top, just like her character on the famous TV show "Laugh In." It was all so surreal and magical. A wonderful time in my life. I was getting to rub elbows and hobnob with all these amazing famous people. But it got even better.

One day my sister called me and asked if I wanted to come to a move premiere in LA. As part of her job at AFI, she often helped with these kinds of events. I said of course I would. Now at the time I owned a green Toyota Camry, not exactly what you would call a sexy car. But it was easy to get dates to go to movie premieres, even in a Toyota Camry. This one time I got this really cute gal to come with me. Because of her good looks and my connection to AFI, I actually got to get in line for the red carpet, which was a huge deal. The movie was a Woody Allen flick called "Sweet and Lowdown," a 1999 American comedy-drama starring Sean Penn as a cocky jazz guitarist who falls for this mute woman. An entertaining but quirky film as you might expect a Woody Allen film to be. Woody was flying in from New York for this event. That was a huge deal because he rarely left New York. So when I drove up in my Camry, Woody Allen's limo was right behind me. I get out with my gorgeous date and people were looking — and I'm sure they are thinking "who's this schmuck with the Camry?"

If you've never been in a Paparazzi line, it's insane. Bright lights flashing everywhere, all the time. Fans screaming from the bleachers and dozens of fans clamoring for autographs. Just absolute human chaos. So I'm walking down the carpet in a trance thinking *"wow, this is what it's like to be famous."* and I hear a photographer shout over to another photographer "who's that?" referring to me. The guy next to him says, "He's nobody." Which was just super. I felt like shit. But my date turns to me and says, "You know what? You're on the red carpet and he's not. Fuck him." I thought, "You know what...she's right." So I held my head up and we went in and watched the movie. As we entered, we saw an amazing spread of food, but what caught my attention was the hotdogs and mashed potatoes stuffed inside Champagne goblets. Yes, you read that correctly. So who is standing next to me eating hot dogs and mashed potatoes from Champagne goblets but Elliot Gould. I was so nervous, as he was another of my favorite actors.

There we were shooting the breeze eating hot dogs and mashed potatoes together — in champagne glasses. Weird but rather revealing.

What I discovered is when you're in "their" world behind closed doors, they're just like you and me. I have insecurities and anxiety. But so do they. In fact, I would say it's not a stretch to say even more so. Some insanely so because they're always looking for their next gig. I remember talking to Michael Dorn who I had met and become friends with. For those who may not recognize the name, Michael is the actor who played Worf in the Star Trek franchise series and films. He was telling me he actually was in the '70s TV series "Chips" and always felt like he was the token black guy. We would mess around with him when people were around. Once when we were chatting, I said, so what was your line in the show, something like, "Yeah, Ponch." That's Oscar material. He turned to me and said, "Fuck you" and we all laughed our asses off. So real. At one of Natalie's parties I rang the doorbell and Michael York answered. It just blew me away to swim in those waters for a while. But what I discovered is they are no different than you and me. They are just people. And people have their problems, which brings me to my ex-wife and lost Emmy Awards.

My second marriage didn't work out. Even though I had a "real" job, it wasn't enough. I suspected other causes but that's not important. We were broken and she asked me to move out and move out right away. Which I did. I got an apartment about an hour-and-a-half away in Seal Beach. Now I had a bunch of my stuff in the three-car garage of our small house in Valencia. Remember, there are no basements in LA, so a lot my stuff was stored in boxes out in the garage, which Melinda was kind enough to let me keep. About two months later I went down to Valencia to collect some of my belongings but was shocked to see about half my boxes were gone. I asked her what happened to them, and she told me she wasn't sure I was ever going to come back for them, so she threw them away. Including the box with my four Emmy Awards. I remember several times over the next few years contacting *The National Academy of Television Arts & Sciences* (NATAS) to see about getting replacement awards. Unfortunately, there wasn't a replacement category for when your ex-wife throws away your awards. Years later I was having dinner with the president of the

Midwest NATAS organization who asked me to be a judge for a local competition. As we were having dinner, I told her my sob story about my ex throwing mine away. At the end of the evening, she said "You just can't make up stuff like that. Tell you what, send me the information about each of the awards, the categories and all that stuff and I'll see what I can do." One month later this big, beautiful box shows up at my front door and just like that, I had my replacement statues.

Sometimes things work out even when they don't work out.

CHAPTER 9

"Major Tom To Ground Control: From Launching Rockets To Launching My Company."

I'd like to switch gears a little bit and talk about my career path and how I ended up owning my company. It's been an amazing ride. I have seen and done so much, and everything I did prior to opening the doors to my company had prepared me well for doing this. I had owned a company in the late '80s-early '90s, so I knew what to expect and how to get if off the ground for the most part. I had climbed the proverbial corporate ladder at each of my previous "career" positions, most of which were very successful; a few not so much. All in all I gained an immense amount of knowledge, things you could never learn in school, all of it unique. Very niche stuff. The kind of experience and expertise you can only get working with experienced pros and a little trial and error.

In the next few chapters, I am going to get into detail about the places I have worked and how they each contributed to my growth, first as a marketer, then as an Orals Coach, and finally as a business owner serving the defense community and federal government at large. Along the way I will also share how my ongoing battle with anxiety played into both my relationships and my professional work.

My first position in the defense/aerospace industry was with Rockwell Aerospace, which at the time was located in Chula Vista, California. It was a huge step in a major new direction for me professionally. I failed as an actor in Hollywood, but on my second trip to LA I got this job just prior to my second divorce. I had started a successful film/video company and had a background in doing video for marketing, but this was to be a totally different experience. I was put in charge of marketing for the NASA Space Shuttle. At the time, Rockwell had a lock on this contract with NASA, and it was a massive contract. I started out doing routine marketing stuff but was then asked to specifically work on marketing for the Space Shuttle. Rockwell had earned its reputation early on as Rockwell Manufacturing Company making industrial valves, German 2-cycle motors, power tools, gas and water meters. In 1973 it was combined with aerospace products and renamed Rockwell International. We still called it Rockwell Aerospace because that was our niche. Where I worked was intimidating at first. As a kid I had wanted to be an astronaut and had even written NASA a letter and had received a response. More about that later.

So here I was, at ground zero for the U.S. Space Shuttle and Apollo rocket research, engineering and manufacturing facility. It was a community unto itself, a massive complex situated on several hundred acres near Downey, California, right there where they built the entire Apollo Command and Service Module.

Through a Rockwell-owned company called Rocketdyne, we also built space rocket engines. Specifically, they built the powerful F1 engines for the Saturn V rocket which was a big deal which revolutionized space travel. The F1 engine had been in the works for a long time. It was originally developed as a successor to the E1 engine commissioned by the U.S. Air Force in the mid-to-late 1950s but abandoned after several failures. The Air Force also soon abandoned the F1 engine because it saw no need for such a massive engine. Years later however, NASA would revive the program and ask for improvements to the F1 because in it they saw a way to power their modules into space. The Saturn V was developed under the Apollo space program specifically for NASA's human exploration of the moon. It was a huge success and later, it was instrumental as the primary engine for Skylab, the first American space station.

This was the place where all the magic was made, and I was a kid in a dream-come-true candy store. People don't realize how much of the space program has its roots in that part of California. I certainly didn't know the entire space shuttle fleet was built in Downey, CA. I always thought it was built in Florida at Cape Canaveral where they launch the rockets and the Johnson Space Center in Houston because that's where mission control was — "Houston, we have a problem." But nope, it was in Downey, CA. And I was there in the thick of what was going on from 1995 to 1999.

One of the things I discovered working there is we also had the world's largest clean room. A clean room is a highly protected and sterilized environment where you have to wear what they call a bunny suit. They can't take any chances of *anything* contaminating the work they are doing. Believe me, they are very strict with these protocols and don't mess around. The suits look goofy, but they actually eliminate airborne particulates by using certain kinds of HEPA (high-efficiency particulate absorbing) filters that remove something on the order of 99.7% of dust, pollen, mold, bacteria, and any airborne particles.

Working at the epicenter of the shuttle program brought me into a lot of cool places and I met a lot of super smart people. One of the places we would frequently go to is Edwards Air Force Base which is home to the Air Force Test Center, Pilot School, and NASA's Armstrong Flight Research Center. You might be familiar with it because Chuck Yeager broke the sound barrier there in the Bell X-1 which was a rocket engine-powered aircraft. It was also home to the first landings of the space shuttle. The base sits in a desert valley. The drive from LA is gorgeous. You go up in the mountains and when you get to the other side, it just appears out of the salt flats. One of the things I noticed right away is the number of completely black buildings. No building signs. No numbers. Nothing except signs on the perimeters that read "Restricted Area. Use of Deadly Force Authorized". These buildings are where the military is working on top secret new programs — they are scattered all across the area.

Among those buildings was this huge hangar, and inside of that was where we did all the shuttle upgrades. I got to see the shuttle shell for the first time when I went there. Before you can visit, you have to go through a two-hour debrief on what you can and can't do around it. As we headed out of the debrief and toward the hanger, I had goosebumps on my arms. When I walked in and saw it for the first time, I broke down crying. I saw my baby. I saw my first spaceship in real life. It was an unreal experience. Seeing the space shuttle blew me away, but there were lots of things like that I got to see and experience first-hand. For one thing, the Apollo 14 command module was right outside my office. THE REAL THING WAS SITTING RIGHT OUTSIDE MY OFFICE! It was the most amazing facility you could possibly imagine. My office had artifacts from everything including from the Apollo program—posters, pins, space suits. I even had a docking hatch from the Apollo Soyuz mission. It was sitting in a closet down from my office. I took it out and brought it to my office. I was now the custodian of all this stuff. We were the NASA storage facility. We held all this stuff. That's what Rockwell Aerospace, this Downey facility, was, in large measure. It was all owned by NASA. We were simply the caretakers. In its heyday, there were about 60,000 people working there. Keep in mind, this was before computers became commonplace. Which means the vast majority of everything was designed on drafting tables. There were CAD/CAM programs. It was all manual so there were warehouses four and five stories tall with wooden arched ceilings — as far as the eye could see (about the size of two football fields). There were huge open areas with row upon row of drafting tables lined up. There were also two-story shelved bookcases on wheels. These guys would do their eight hour drafting shifts and when they were done, they would wheel out the shelving tables and the next group would come in and continue drawing … and so it went around the clock.

Another thing I remember is the full-scale mockup of the Orbiter in the DEI room, or the Design Engineering Institute room. This was a huge room that held several thousand people. In the middle of this room was this behemoth model with wooden panels. If the panels were raised on its side, you could see this labyrinth of colored string running the length of it. This is how they measured for the wiring they would eventually need. Tons of it — enough to wrap around the Earth three times.

The facilities were very cool, but what was cooler were the people. My journey as an Orals Coach really began in earnest at Rockwell. I have many fond memories of working with the astronauts. They taught me a lot. I was like a sponge. I had already earned a reputation about being detail-oriented and that trait kicked into a higher gear during this time. I wanted to know everything about everything. Like I was a scientist. That was a big deal for me. I became immersed in how the shuttle shell worked and every system and subsystem — I was an info maniac. I asked everybody, please tell me this, please tell me that. I mean I was lucky enough to work in this rarified space and I wanted to completely take advantage of it because I was working with the people who designed it.

I worked with lot of the Apollo engineers. There was a funny aside about these guys. I went to see Apollo 13, the movie, which had been released during this time. I went to see it with a bunch of the guys who designed that very stuff. In one scene there's an explosion, and the side blows out of the service module. We were all sitting in a row at the theater at the Downey facility watching this thing. The second the explosion happened on screen, they all said, "Oh, please. You can't hear anything in a vacuum!" I laughed and said, "Guys, it's a movie. You know? Not a documentary." We all laughed. Anyway, I got to meet the astronauts. During this time I also learned about the Silver Snoopy awards, which aren't a widely known thing. The Silver Snoopys' are little, tiny Snoopy pins. Charles Schultz was a space fanatic. He loved space and there's a whole series of animated cells he did for Snoopy with the big helmet on. He carried them all the way to the shuttle program to give to the astronauts who then took them to space shuttle, and come back down with them. They would then be awarded to associates who went above and beyond the call of duty to support the space program. An employee would be at a cubicle and suddenly, an astronaut in a blue jumpsuit would come around the corner with a press guy and he would say, "Hey, so and so, stand up," and that person would be pinned. They usually would invite the family to be there when it happened. There would be a photo op, and the astronaut would pin this space-flown Snoopy pin on the recipient and present the winner with a certificate. People cherished that stuff. I was part of the communication team who would put this together, so we knew it was coming. One time, the head of the space program received one and that was pretty cool. At that time, four people were getting awards and he was the fifth person to receive one. He had no idea about it, and got very emotional.

During my time at Rockwell, I got to go to Cape Canaveral and watch a few rocket launches. I rode up the gantry elevator to the walkway where the white or "clean" room was located. This is where a final check is given before they enter the capsule which is fully loaded, fueled and ready to go. These were experiences most people could only dream of. I had watched launches when I was a kid and would get emotional, but actually being there and feeling it is otherworldly. Just extraordinary.

Once the astronauts are in the capsule, everybody leaves and the closest a spectator can be is four miles away. If something horrible should happen, shrapnel would fly out for miles. To understand just how far that really is, I would tell people to get in their car and drive four miles — think about it. Most people can't fathom that. But hearing it and feeling the thunder and roar of a space rocket lifting off is a tremendously powerful experience. It's just an amazing thing to watch. I would think to myself, *"I just watched a rocket go up with seven people inside hurtling skyward with the ass end just one big ball of flames beneath them."*

Watching them return to Earth was equally astounding. Keep in mind, the Shuttle Landing Facility at Cape Canaveral covers 500 acres and has a single runway, one of the longest in the world at 15,000 feet, and 300 feet wide. It is a truly amazing feat of

engineering in and of itself. The materials used the groove design
— everything is meticulously designed and built to withstand
extremely high temperatures, weight, and to help maximize the
braking ability of the Shuttle. It's known by the local workers as
a "gator tanning facility," as some of the 4,000 alligators at the
center regularly bask in the sunlight on the runway.

While watching my first shuttle landing. I was looking off into
the horizon to see if I could spot the shuttle as it was coming in
from space. One of the shuttle workers tapped me on the shoulder
and said, "Schiffy, look" as he pointed way up over my shoulder.
Then I saw it. It came in at a 37-degree angle and I heard the sonic
"boom" as it began to corkscrew into the atmosphere to disburse
energy. Not even 50 minutes ago, they were going 18,000 miles
an hour yet when they approach to land, they are going about 140
miles per hour — coming to a dead stop with a parachute being
deployed in the final moments. It's incredible to see in real life and
I was standing there, my jaw open with a stunned "Wow!" look
on my face. I thought, *"There are people in that thing!"* In fact,
in the last few thousand feet, those people are flying that machine.
How it could be completely automated, yet the astronauts want
to fly and land that spacecraft. It's just crazy. So getting a chance
to work on the program, meet the designers, work crews and the
astronauts was simply one of the greatest thrills of my life. Never,
in my wildest dreams as a kid, did I ever think I would experience
this, work on the program, and meet the astronauts. For a kid who
wanted to be an astronaut, it was a dream come true.

This brings me to the story I mentioned earlier about writing
a letter to NASA. When I was 11 years old, I wrote a letter to

NASA. At the time Apollo 15 was going to be landing on the moon in a place called Hadley Rille. This was a feature of the lunar landscape named from nearby Mons Hadley. Scientist believe it is likely that the channel was carved into the surface by volcanic processes earlier in its history. I wrote a letter my parents helped me type.

It read:

"Dear NASA, when the astronauts land at Hadley's Rille, please tell them to be careful because when the crater shook it probably made the ground really loose and I don't want them to trip and fall."

A few weeks later, I got a letter back from NASA saying, "David, your observations are highly astute, so stay in school and maybe one day you can work in NASA." And that was that. I became a director, never imagining I would work with NASA. Then 20 years later, there I was, working with NASA and rubbing elbows with astronauts. At one point during this time, I actually applied to the astronaut program and made the first round of cuts because I had been sponsored by friends at NASA. But that's a whole other series of stories. I told my parents that, possibly, I may be an astronaut after all …maybe a mission payload specialist or something like that since I wasn't a pilot. Well, I flunked out. But I wasn't bummed. It was exciting just to have been a part of that whole scene. My time at Rockwell right until Boeing bought the company were the best years of my life. I had gone from being a director to launching a whole new career in the defense and aerospace industries.

I learned the craft of presenting to the government. I began to cut my teeth in a serious way making and delivering presentations. Teaching others how to give their oral arguments to the evaluators. It was the beginning of a significant sea change in my career and paved the way to starting The Schiff Group. I will never forget those days of my life.

The stage had been set and I was ready for the next leading role in my career.

CHAPTER 10

"It's A Secret. And People Can Die If You Aren't Careful With It."

I'm going to change gears here for a moment and talk a little about what it's like working for the government — the military/ DOD (Department of Defense) in particular. To be more specific, I want to tell you a couple of stories about what it's like obtaining a government security clearance and working in highly secure environments … and why I believe it's a solemn responsibility and not something to fuck around with. Getting cleared to have access to our country's secrets is a big deal and most people don't really understand all that is at stake.

While I risk stating the obvious, getting cleared to work in secure environments isn't something you just apply for and get. Obtaining a security clearance isn't easy and not everyone who applies will be granted access. Not by a long shot. The requirements are stringent, and you have to be deemed suitable on a number of levels, especially when working in the intelligence community as I have for more than 25 years.

First, you don't just apply for yourself. The company you work for has to get the ball rolling. Most people who know anything about clearances are familiar with three basic levels of security classification:

- **Confidential**: This clearance refers to material which, if improperly disclosed, could be reasonably expected to cause some measurable damage to national security. The vast majority of military personnel are given this very basic level of clearance. It must be reinvestigated every 15 years.
- **Secret:** Unauthorized disclosure of the information this clearance covers could be expected to cause grave damage to national security. This level gets reinvestigated every 10 years.
- **Top Secret**: Individuals with this clearance have access to information or material expected to cause exceptionally grave damage to national security if it is released without authorization. This level is reinvestigated every five years.

However, this is the tip of the iceberg when it comes to *highly* sensitive information. In these cases, even higher security clearances are granted in order to allow military members, federal employees, and contractors access to sensitive information, facilities, or circumstances, these clearances are not granted lightly and must not be taken for granted. Without going too deep down this rabbit hole, here's the basic outline of what are known as Special Access Programs /Special Access Required (SAP/SAR) access which is where I have done a great deal of my work.

SAP/SAR access is only offered to certain qualifying federal employees or uniformed service members who are recommended for the program. You are *not* automatically approved to participate in a Special Access Program just because you carry a Secret clearance or better. You must be nominated, your security clearance investigation must have taken place in the last five years, and the following are also required. Applicant must:

- Take a random Counterintelligence (CI) — scope polygraph examination when required.
- Sign a DOD-approved SAP program indoctrination.
- Sign a non-disclosure agreement.
- Acknowledge that violations of the NDA may lead to termination of access, removal from a position of special confidence, and prosecution.
- Acknowledge the NDA is in perpetuity.

So that's a little primer on security clearances. Now here are a few brief stories of my experiences in this arena.

When I started at Rockwell Aerospace and launched my new career as an Orals Coach helping defense contractors learn and rehearse presentations outlining their qualifications and arguments for winning government contracts, little did I know what that actually involved, including getting cleared to view and handle classified documents and materials. For those not familiar with security clearances, there are several levels of clearance ranging from Confidential to Secret, Top Secret and several even much higher than that. Of course, this was all new to me and I have to say it's a bit intimidating to go through this process.

It all starts with the SF86 (Security Form 86) which everyone must fill out when requesting government security clearances. Basically, it's telling your life story. The security clearance process typically includes an FBI reference check of former employers, coworkers, friends, neighbors, landlords, and schools along with a review of credit, tax, police records and more. The scope of the background investigation varies depending on the level of clearance requested/required. It's a painful process to go through. You have to remember names, places, addresses. All of the stuff I just mentioned. But here's a funny little aside.

Standard Form 86
Revised September 1995
U.S. Office of Personnel Management
5 CFR Parts 731, 732, and 736

Form approved:
OMB No. 3206-0007
NSN 7540-00-634-4036
86-111

Questionnaire for National Security Positions

Follow instructions fully or we cannot process your form. Be sure to sign and date the certification statement on Page 9 and the release on Page 10. *If you have any questions*, call the office that gave you the form.

Purpose of this Form
The U.S. Government conducts background investigations and reinvestigations to establish that military personnel, applicants for or incumbents in national security positions, either employed by the Government or working for Government contractors, licensees, certificate holders, and grantees, are eligible for a required security clearance. Information from this form is used primarily as the basis for investigation for access to classified information or special nuclear information or material. Complete this form only after a conditional offer of employment has been made for a position requiring a security clearance.

Giving us the informatio~~n~~ voluntary. However, we may not be able to comple~~te~~ or complete it in a timely manner, if you don't ~~give~~ ormation we request. This may affect your place~~ment~~ e prospects.

Authority to Request
Depending upon the pur~~pose~~ tigation, the U.S. Government is authorized to ask for this ~~inf~~ on under Executive Orders 10450, 10865, 12333, and 12356; sections 3301 and 9101 of title 5, U.S. Code; sections 2165 and 2201 of title 42, U.S. Code; sections 781 to 887 of

You may also be asked to bring documents about information you provided on the form or other matters requiring specific attention. These matters include alien registration, delinquent loans or taxes, bankruptcy, judgments, liens, or other financial obligations, agreements involving child custody or support, alimony or property settlements, arrests, convictions, probation, and/or parole.

Organization of this Form

This form has two parts. Part 1 asks for background information, including where you have lived, gone to school, and worked. Part 2 asks about your activities and such matters as firings from a job, criminal history record, use of illegal drugs, and abuse of alcohol.

In answering all questions on this form, keep in mind that your answers are considered together with the information obtained in the investigation to reach an appropriate adjudication.

Instructions for Completing this Form
1. Follow the instructions given to you by the person who gave you the form and any other clarifying instructions furnished by that person to assist you in completion of the form. Find out how many copies of the

In this particular case I was at Northrop Grumman, and I was preparing to get my Top-Secret clearance, an upgrade from the Secret clearance. It's a big deal. So I filled out all the paperwork going back seven years and submitted it. Not long after, a couple of FBI investigators came by my office at Northrup for some follow up and final questions in person. They needed some clarification on a few of my responses. In filling out my form, I had mentioned my Uncle Alex, Dad's brother who lives in New Zealand. I couldn't remember his address so I left that blank. Obviously, a big red flag. So these guys are in my office asking me about it. I told them I couldn't recall, but perhaps my mom has the information, and would it be okay if I call her while you guys are here. They said sure. So I called up Mom who has a very heavy Hungarian accent and doesn't understand any of this kind of stuff in the least. And, of course, my mom is quite the character.

She answered the phone saying, "Hello dahlink" sounding all Zsa Gaborish.

I said, "Hey Mom, do you remember when I told you I was going through a security clearance investigation and you might be interviewed and asked some questions?"

"Yes, they talked to me the other day," she replied.

"Well, Mom, they need Uncle Alex's address," I said.

Without missing a beat she blurts out in a dismissive tone, "Oh honey, I wouldn't use him as a reference."

The FBI agents, normally stoic and all business, just cracked up. Still laughing, one of the agents said, "Mrs. Schiff, we just need his address to verify who he is."

So Mom says, "Oh. Well, my husband and I are not very close with him."

By this time, the agents are desperately trying to control their laughter. I interrupted and said "Mom, could you please just give these folks his address, please?" It was absolutely hilarious.

Another time when I was at Rockwell Aerospace, I had just obtained my first Secret Clearance. Now if you have ever had the privilege of getting a clearance, there are people who take it for granted, and others who take it very seriously. I was a nerd who took it all *very* seriously. I view it as an honor to have access to and to review classified material. Believe me, it's very true when they say that in the wrong hands, this information can lead to bad things. Which brings me to the moment I had given my final signature and was approved for my Secret clearance. We were about to head into a meeting, and I was really excited about going into this room. Like it was some kind of James Bond thing, right? It just so happens the guy who had approved my very first clearance at Rockwell Aerospace years before handed me a folder and said, "Before you go into this room, I wanted you to look at this first." He handed me a folder with a newspaper article inside. The headline read:

"Two Soldiers in a Covert Mission in Colombia Killed by Cartel"

I looked at him and said, "Okay…."

He said, "How do you feel about that story?"

My response was that it was horrible, but to be honest I had become desensitized to stuff like that because it seemed to be all over the news all the time. I wasn't all that surprised something like that had happened.

With no expression, he said to me in a chilling, matter-of-fact tone, "What if I were to tell you the information you're going to be seeing today in the wrong hands could have led to the death of these two people?"

Well, that just floored me completely. I was really taken aback.

Then he said to me, "I want you to think about two things every time you go into a meeting like this."

1. Do I need to see this stuff?
2. How do I protect it with my life?

It hit me like a ton of bricks, and I looked at him and said, "I get it." Ever since that day, when I would go into a SCIF meeting, I would think about those two things. Pronounced "Skiff," SCIF stands for Sensitive Compartmented Information Facility, a U.S. Department of Defense term for a secure room where classified materials are being viewed, discussed and handled by meeting participants. Often, since then, there have been moments when I was exposed to things which are a little bit on the scary side — you lose sleep here and there because you have the information inside your head. At least I did, because it's just a fact there are people and entities out there who will do all kinds of things to get the information. This is the real deal; you have an obligation as a person who gets exposure to sensitive information, including some of the nation's top defense secrets, to be ultra-responsible with it.

One of the clearances I had which was probably the scariest in terms of responsibility was called CNWDI which stands for Critical Nuclear Weapon Design Information. We pronounced it Sin Widdy. As you might imagine, this clears you to view and handle information related to a range of nuclear weapons information, from theories of operation to actual design of nuclear warheads, and demolition munition and test devices, among other things. Now I didn't necessarily want to have this clearance, but I had to have it in order to do the kinds of presentations I was required to do for my job. It was scary stuff. The kind of information a whole lot of people would love to get their hands on. It was scary as hell at first, but I grew to understand my responsibilities and was proud to be among a select few in the know about this stuff.

Now there were times when I witnessed breaches of security. I was sometimes shocked and saddened at how some people took this stuff for granted and either deliberately or through carelessness mishandled government secrets.

One time after a Skiff briefing, we were leaving, and I saw this guy carrying a manila folder half open as he left the meeting. I could see it had floppy discs inside that were marked Secret. I asked the guy "What are you doing with those?"

He replied, "I'm just going back to my office."

I said, "Yeah, but those discs aren't sealed. I can see them from here."

"Oh, it doesn't matter," he said.

"Well, yeah it does. You're not supposed to do that," I shot back.

He looked at me with a smart-ass look and said, "Well you don't have to make a big stink about it."

I calmly replied, "You can walk back into the Skiff right now and I'll just file a report that you made a mistake. If you keep walking, I'm going to file a different kind of report."

He looked at me and yelled, "Why are you being such an asshole about this?"

"I'm not being an asshole," I said. "These are the guidelines you and I have to live by."

He looked at me and walked back into the briefing room and sealed up the discs. To this day I know I did the right thing. This stuff needs to be taken seriously.

Another story which comes to mind was a defense contractor's office I was working at. It involved a competitor of mine. There were two copy machines in this controlled section of the building. One was for classified material and the other was for unclassified material. You just didn't copy classified information on the unclassified machine because the classified copiers had a memory card to record and keep track of what was being copied. There's more to it, but you get the idea.

So I am watching this guy copy secret documents on the wrong machine and I walked over to him and said, "What are you doing?"

"That's none of your business," he said.

"Um, yeah, actually it is," I said. "You're copying classified documents on the unclassified copy machine and now we have to call facilities and security because they have to scrub that machine now."

"You don't know what the fuck you're talking about," he barked back to me."

"Yeah, I kinda do," I said.

So I immediately called security and these two big guys in uniforms show up, take away the guy's badge and escort him out of the building.

Evidently, I did know what the fuck I was talking about. I don't get any joy from this kind of thing, it's just that I'm a strict advocate about the importance of security. Otherwise, what the hell is the point?

Now, here's something that will make your hair stand on end. It happened during the time I worked at a company called Leidos. Leidos is an American defense, aviation, information technology company headquartered in Reston, Virginia that provides scientific, engineering, systems integration, and technical services to the government.

At that time in 2016, I was working on a program for the National Security Agency (NSA), and I had just seen the Oliver Stone film "Snowden." The movie details the exploits of Edward Snowden, a former computer intelligence consultant who leaked highly classified information from NSA in 2013 when he was an employee and subcontractor for the CIA.

I was at NSA headquarters just making conversation with some of the guys in the room and I said to this one guy, "Hey, have you ever seen the movie Snowden?" Suddenly and collectively all these heads turned around to stare at me like I was some sinister, evil person. Well, it turns out THESE were the guys who had to clean up the mess Snowden had created, and it was a very, very sore subject with them.

I'll never forget when they told me, "David, when you are given a clearance and do anything even close to what he did, that's treason. It's a capital offense." I said it was just a movie, and they all shook their heads and one guy said, "What he did was horribly wrong, and it needs to be corrected."

I was floored and red in the face. But boy did I get their message loud and clear.

Okay, so enough with the super serious stuff. Sometimes along the way you encounter some pretty funny situations. Not always at the time they are happening, but in retrospect, pretty funny stuff.

One day I was in a highly classified meeting in a skiff — actually a skiff within a skiff. That's how secret this meeting was. There are no clocks, or phones or other communications devices allowed in the skiff. Everybody else had left and I was alone in the room working and lost track of time. I needed to use the bathroom, which is about a three-minute walk to get to from the sealed rooms I was working in. Unbeknownst to me, while I was gone for a few minutes, the security officer, thinking nobody was left in the building, locked the skiff up tight and went through the lockdown protocol, going down the hall and checking everything to make sure all was secure. Then he turned on the alarm and motion sensors which are all over the place. I left the first room, went through the second room, and opened the door to the hallway — there's a security cop there with his gun drawn on me. I had tripped the motion sensors.

I said, "What the fuck?"

"What are you doing here?" he asked.

I told him I was just working. He rolled his eyes and told me now he has to call the head of security, who I knew. A few minutes later he arrives and says, "Schiffy, I'm sorry. We thought you were gone."

I about wet my pants right there and then. Not something you want to see trying to go out a door to take a leak.

I'll share one more with you my friends in the business never let me forget.

Years ago I had bought a Tesla. I loved that car. I thought it was cool and thought I was cool for having it. During this time I was doing work for NSA at Fort Meade, Maryland. As you might imagine, this is a pretty high-security facility, and they don't mess around. In fact, in 2015 a man was shot to death by NSA police trying to run the gate in an unauthorized vehicle.

One day while I was working there, we took a break. I was hungry for a Subway sandwich as I had seen people coming into the office with Subway bags at lunch time. I asked my colleagues where the nearest Subway was.

"Just go out of the parking lot and make a right, take your next right and it's right there. Just follow the road around the strip mall and you can't miss it," they said.

So out I went with one of my buddies. I exited the lot, made a right and suddenly I see these fence lines with the government warnings on them. You know, the kind that if you cross, they'll shoot you. I told my buddy I thought I made a wrong turn. So I turn around and head for the gate and there standing in front of us is a guard with her automatic weapon in hand. She asked if she could help me, so I told her what I was trying to do and handed her my badge with my company information. I asked if I could make a U turn. She told me that was fine, but they had to run a check on me first. I later found out they had recently had an intrusion and the facility was on a heightened state of alert.

Understandable and no problem. Or so I thought.

The incursion she was referring to was only two days prior. Two men had tried to run the gate, both wearing women's clothing. It was kind of a big deal and had been reported in the news. I pulled around and another guard came up with his pistol holstered and asked me for my driver's license, which I gave him.

About a minute later he comes back, gun drawn and tells me, "Sir, you need to get out of the car right now. I need to handcuff you." Well, this was unexpected and really freaked me out. I asked him what the hell he was talking about, and he said my license was listed as suspended and to step out of my vehicle.

Well, it turns out it was a mistake by the bank about a payment that didn't go through. I can't really remember exactly what the problem was. But federal law requires gate guards to apprehend anyone with a suspended license attempting to access federal property because it is actually a felony. False identification. Great.

I get out of my car, and the guard tells me to sit on the curb. Remember me telling you I almost wet my pants? Yeah, it was close again this time. I asked if the handcuffs were really necessary. At this point I am pretty freaked out.

"No," he said, "probably not, but I have to seize your license and you cannot drive that vehicle. Your friend will have to drive but we also have to run a check on your vehicle. Please open up your trunk. "

Now, Teslas don't have an engine, but they DO have a trunk **and** a "frunk" which is a trunk in the front. This seemed to confuse the hell out of this guard. He brings the dog around to sniff and he looks bewildered and says to me, "I have no idea what kind of car this is," as he had never seen a Tesla before. He finished up the inspection and tells me to stand up in front of the fence so he can take my photograph for security report purposes. Once he was done, he released us. I'm shaking like a leaf from the experience, and I tell the guy I am with (I was his boss) he better not mention this incident to anybody back at the office because it was just so embarrassing — even though I didn't do anything wrong. We walk into the office of the company I was working for and there were like 20 people in the room and in unison, they all held up their hands together with their wrists touching and their fingers spread out like they were handcuffed laughing hysterically.

"How did you guys know about this" I asked.

It turns out two of the guys in the room had driven by us while I was sitting on the curb in handcuffs and thought it was hilarious to go back and tell everybody.

My point in all of this is the government takes security very seriously and there is no room for breaches of any kind. Even if you have one of the highest clearances possible, minor things like trying to enter a federal facility with a suspended license can get you sitting on a curb in handcuffs.

Oh, by the way, I never got my fucking Subway sandwich.

CHAPTER 11

"Just Relax"

I f you suffer from anxiety — even a little — that phrase is the singular, most annoying thing a person can ever say to you. Just relax. Really? Oh, I'm sorry I have anxiety and it's difficult to manage, but okay, I'll "just relax."

Overcoming anxiety is possible. Managing it is critical to people in the communications business — especially if you are standing in front of a group of grizzled government evaluators judging your every word, movement and nuance of a presentation potentially worth hundreds of millions of dollars or more to your company. It can be traumatic and devastating and I have seen it all first-hand. In this chapter I will share what it means to be an Orals Coach and some of the stories I have been part of over the past couple of decades in this business.

What I do for a living is unique and fairly unusual in the business world. I am an Orals Coach, which doesn't mean much to those who aren't in my line of work. So I'd like to take some time to explain what I do, and then relate some stories about what this job has meant to me personally and professionally, and how people have reacted to me along this journey.

So, what is an Orals Coach? Those outside my world may often think Orals Coaches teach people how to be effective public speakers. That couldn't be further from the truth of what we do. Our job is NOT to help you become an effective public speaker. In fact the word "public" has nothing to do with what we do. Neither does "speaking" to be honest. An Orals Coach isn't somebody who helps you get up in front of a crowd of people in a public setting and make speeches. Frankly, a phrase more apropos to describe what we do is help our clients become "private presenters." This is true for two main reasons: First, our clients are doing their business in very private (most often government classified) settings in closed rooms few people ever enter, much less know about. Secondly, our clients are not "speaking," they are presenting a case their company is making to government evaluators who hold the keys to a thumbs up or thumbs down decision to award massive government contracts to their company — anything from satellite communications to the most sophisticated military technology in the world. Do it right and we can help our clients hire hundreds, even thousands of employees and make hundreds of millions of dollars. Do it wrong and the very survival of some companies might be at stake.

Now let's take a look at what Oral Proposal Presentations are. Orals presentations can be either live in-person or in real-time video conferencing via secured communications channels. I have to mention that it's key to understand Orals Presentations are just a part of the overall presentation and submission process potential government contractors must undergo when pursuing these types of lucrative new business opportunities with the government.

Long before our clients ever get in front of government evaluators, they have spent as long as two years — sometimes more — preparing for a face-to-face meeting. They have been qualified to receive, been issued and put together their responses to excruciatingly detailed RFPs (Request For Proposal). If they are lucky enough to check off all those boxes, government evaluators may choose them to give a live presentation to help sort the competition and arrive at their final contenders. This is when the government has the opportunity to meet the actual Program Managers and staff; see how they perform under pressure, evaluate their knowledge and the depth of their grasp of the concepts, content at hand, and determine if they would be a comfortable fit on both a personal as well as a professional level. During an

Orals presentation, the evaluators will get a first-hand "feel" for their potential contract team. It's a big deal. It's human nature for the evaluators to want to "like" the presenters. Which is fair. After all, they will be spending long hours over several years working on these huge projects. So the Orals part of the entire process is a major factor in making the final award decision.

That's where my company, The Schiff Group, has earned our stripes over the years. Our team is comprised of subject matter experts (SME) and business strategists, but we also have deep expertise in marketing, communications, film, television, and video production.

We know what it takes to help our clients command whatever stage they are on during an Orals Proposal Presentation. It all needs to be carefully choreographed. The chemistry has to be just right. The charts and other supporting material you use must be thoughtfully created, planned and positioned. The blocking and staging have to be smooth. The transitions and handoffs have to be friendly and seamless. The language must be fluid and conversational. The physical gestures have to be natural and engaging. You have to be prepared to be "good on your feet" and confident when questions are asked.

All of this and much more is what makes for an effective presentation. Yet the challenges can be overwhelming for many people. Just consider these challenging dynamics:

- You will spend long, often highly stressful hours to prepare
- There's a strict time limit: usually no more than 90 minutes
- There usually are multiple presenters with very different personalities and styles
- The slides are often prepared by Small and Medium Enterprises, not the presenters themselves
- All content is usually highly technical and has to be presented conversationally
- You have to be prepared for a Q&A and think on your feet
- Some people have never had to do this and get VERY anxious and stressed out

These dynamics can present tough challenges for the best professionals who are not used to making high-visibility, game-changing presentations. I don't care how good you are at your job in terms of dotting the i's and crossing the t's, if you haven't had much experience in making the kinds of in-person connections Orals require, you might shut down completely. I have seen it time and time again — and it will show when it's Go Time.

My job is to get to know these talented professionals personally, to understand their underlying anxiety and find ways to coax from them what makes them comfortable. I look for ways to work with them well in advance of the time they will "hit the stage" for their big presentation. That is never actually easy to do.

The National Institute for Mental Health (NIMH) categorizes anxiety in three basic categories:

- generalized anxiety disorder (GAD)
- panic disorder
- various phobia-related disorders

According to the NIMH:

People with generalized anxiety disorder (GAD) display excessive anxiety or worry, most days for at least 6 months, about a number of things such as personal health, work, social interactions, and everyday routine life circumstances. The fear and anxiety can cause significant problems in areas of their life, such as social interactions, school, and work.

Generalized anxiety disorder symptoms include:

- Feeling restless, wound-up, or on-edge
- Being easily fatigued
- Having difficulty concentrating; mind going blank

- Being irritable
- Having muscle tension
- Difficulty controlling feelings of worry
- Having sleep problems, such as difficulty falling or staying asleep, restlessness, or unsatisfying sleep

Panic Disorder

People with panic disorder have recurrent unexpected panic attacks. Panic attacks are sudden periods of intense fear that come on quickly and reach their peak within minutes. Attacks can occur unexpectedly or can be brought on by a trigger, such as a feared object or situation.

During a panic attack, people may experience:

- Heart palpitations, a pounding heartbeat, or an accelerated heart rate
- Sweating
- Trembling or shaking
- Sensations of shortness of breath, smothering, or choking
- Feelings of impending doom
- Feelings of being out of control

People with panic disorder often worry about when the next attack will happen, and actively try to prevent future attacks by avoiding places, situations, or behaviors they associate with panic attacks. Worry about panic attacks, and the effort spent trying to avoid attacks, cause significant problems in various areas of the person's life, including the development of agoraphobia, or the fear of going outside one's home.

I have had all of these in my life at some point and to various degrees. It's not pretty and it can bring you to your knees. I know my personal and professional life with this, and my undying sympathy and compassion for people who have experienced these awful feelings has made me the person — and the professional Orals Coach — I am today.

Now let's talk about what I do in more detail. The key word here is detail. You would not believe how many people I have either coached or encountered in the course of coaching who failed to clearly understand detail. At The Schiff Group, we want our work to be unimpeachable. It has to be, because the presentations our clients ultimately make to their government evaluators has to be unimpeachable. You can never attain perfection. Practice will never make perfect, but it *will* make you better. That may sound like a no-brainer, but you would be surprised.

I remember once many years ago I was in a meeting where I got my first taste of what can go wrong when you don't do what the evaluators ask. In their brief to us to answer the RFP, our evaluators had asked the company to create three design concepts for the project. It was fairly complex, scientific stuff and my company went to work diligently designing concepts. In an attempt to impress the evaluators with the hope of winning the contract, they decided to exceed expectations and came up with no fewer than 21 design concepts which the company had submitted to our potential client.

Well, we lost the bid. As was customary, we would have an out brief meeting to go over why we lost. This was going to be interesting. I was there just to observe so I sat in one of the chairs against the wall off from the main conference room table where the presentation was taking place. Everyone gathered and the meeting began. Prior to the decision, I had asked our Program Manager (let's call him Roger) why the team decided to go ahead with so many design concepts. Beaming with pride and more than a little condescension, Roger told me, "Oh, I know one of the guys we presented to. I went to college with him. He always wants more." I thought, *"Well, okay."* I mean, what the hell did I know about it, right? It was a whole new world to me then.

There we were: everybody was waiting for the out brief with bated breath. It was common then to have a red light and a green light above the presentation screen on the wall at the end of the table. When the meeting began, the light turned green. During the meeting, if there was anything evaluators wanted to be off the record, they would switch the light from green to red.

The meeting began with the bad news of course. We didn't get the contract and the evaluators began to tell us why in detail. The lead evaluator began, and after a few remarks, he flips the light from green to red, leaned forward on the table and looked over at Roger and said, "Before I continue, Roger, what did you not understand about three?" He just shook his head.

Roger looked offended and they argued for a few minutes. Then the evaluator flipped the light back to green and proceeded to tell us in detail why 21 concepts was absurd, along with other reasons why we failed to make the grade.

As the meeting concluded, my boss put his arm around my shoulder and said, "This is why you push back. Good job." He was referring to my questioning the program manager about why he chose to present 21 ideas instead of the three the government had asked for. It's about compliance. Start there. That's when I fell in love with this new world of presentations, orals coaching, technical demonstrations, and all the things I was about to learn which led me to the success I have achieved today.

I was hooked. I thought this was a wonderful new way for me to use my marketing and presentation skills. All the time I spent putting together huge marketing programs combined with my background in acting, directing and theater.

As time passed, I became keenly aware of the pressure people facing government evaluators can be under. As someone who suffered from anxiety all of my life and who had to find ways to overcome it, I was intimately empathetic to the toll that pressure can take on someone, not just professionally but personally. It can eat a person up inside. I'd like to share a few brief stories to give you an idea of what I mean by that.

Years ago I was working on a gig for IBM, which was vying for a very lucrative contract for the U.S. Navy. The program manager at IBM was a former Navy officer. I met her and we began the process of coaching her for the Orals presentation we were planning. Now this particular presentation was going to be held via video. Video Orals is an integral part of what I do, because it's not always possible for everyone to be in the same locale, much less the same room, for a variety of reasons. Early on in the process, I noticed something just didn't seem right. Something was definitely off with her. Keep in mind I have a pretty good Spidey-sense about these things. Part of what I do is to get to know the people I coach on a personal level as best I can, yet something was bothering her in a big way. She didn't seem to be all there. She was very distracted.

One day early into our coaching sessions, I approached her and asked her if she was okay. She looked at me and just broke down in tears. I was caught off guard because she was a seasoned veteran of the Navy but just appeared so incredibly distraught and wasn't able to focus. I felt so bad for her.

As we talked, I learned both her husband and her father had recently died within one week of each other. Turns out she was really a mess. This had hit her really hard, and she was having difficulty coping with it all. I learned she was the one and only person left to handle all the funeral arrangements because her mother was just inconsolable and could barely function. It was a crushing weight on her mind, soul and body. I could see it in her eyes. In her posture. Her hands would shake. She just wasn't "there."

It was sad to see this decorated veteran and incredibly intelligent human being going through such a really difficult period in her life. I can't imagine the burden she was bearing. Here we were smack dab in the middle of a multi-billion-dollar proposal and she hadn't told anyone she was dealing with all of this inside. And alone.

After I learned about of this, I went home and told my wife. I spent the evening thinking about it and the next day I set up a meeting with her executive management team and told them what was going on. They were shocked because she was "so tough" — or so it seemed to them. I told them what I had witnessed and that unless she was given some time off from the ten-hour days and the pressure she was under, there was no way in hell she was going to get it together in time to give anything resembling a passable presentation to the evaluation team. I asked them to give her at least a week off to deal with her family tragedy. Which they did. She was incredibly grateful, took the time off to make the arrangements she needed to make and just take some mental time off from the enormous pressure, and to comfort her mom as well.

A week later she came back a different person. She seemed alert, much stronger and was ready to dive back into work. We continued our work together and when all was said and done, she did an outstanding job — and IBM won the contract, thanks to the courage and determination she was able to reach and pull from inside. She just needed time.

Sometimes part of my job simply involves getting my clients used to being in front of a camera. Some are very natural. Others are scared to death. I can't tell you how often that alone can send people into a cocoon. I remember one client with team members who had never been in front of a camera. I decided I would do some training to get them used to that kind of new and intimidating environment. I brought in a camera and a teleprompter to help them get used to the equipment, and what it was like to stand there with all this "stuff" around them. One of the ways I would get them to try to loosen up was to turn on the camera and play director by asking them to start talking about their childhoods. The first few had no issues and seemed to take to it telling funny stories about growing up. When it came time for this one woman to talk, she had barely started when she just froze, and immediately broke down and began crying hysterically. It turns out she had suffered horrible child abuse. That was really hard; it tore my guts out. I wasn't prepared at all so we stopped, and I cleared the room and asked her if she wanted to talk about it. She said no and she would be okay but that my question about her childhood triggered a reaction she didn't want to relive. After a while we were able to continue, but that shook me personally for a few days. I realized sometimes we all take things for granted. There really is no "normal" for everybody. All of us are different and we all have "those" things in our past that can be ignited, sometimes more easily than we realize. I realized that to personalize those dynamics isn't always the best way to handle everybody, and adjusted my own coaching technique and human skills to avoid it ever happening again.

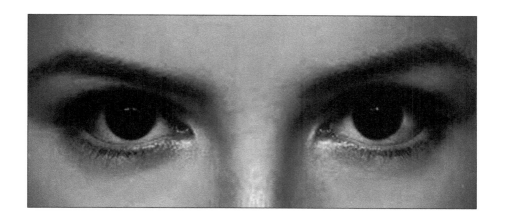

So anxiety, panic and stress can be normal for some, and they can easily handle it, but for others it can be completely debilitating. Here's a case in point — a case where I thought this guy had done something atrocious. In this case, I was doing a prep lecture for a team where I would outline the process, the dynamics and the details of what we were all about to do to prepare for this major Video Orals presentation. We were going to record everybody's part as part of the overall video portion of the presentation. After the lecture, I packed up my stuff and was walking out to the parking lot to my car when this guy came running after me. He said to me, "Hey, Schiffy, you know when you mentioned that if we ever need help to get our heads right for a presentation it's perfectly okay to talk with a therapist?"

"Yes," I replied

"Well, it's not for me. It's my daughter. She's a cutter," he said.

"Oh my god, that's awful," I said.

He then asked me if I thought my own therapist or someone I knew would be open to talking to her because they didn't like the one they had. "Absolutely," I said. I told him I could give him some numbers to call, including my own. He thanked me and we went our separate ways. So a week goes by, and I was talking to my therapist. I asked if this guy had called her. She said no, he hadn't called her. The next week I saw him in the parking lot and asked him why he hadn't called.

He looked at me and said, "What therapist?" I reminded him of our conversations a few weeks back and he said, "Oh, that. Yeah, we're fine now." I was rather taken aback and quizzed him more about it. I thought it was odd he never followed up because any kind of self-harm, particularly cutting, is a big deal and she should probably get help right away. As we continued talking, I got the sense this man was lying to me. I asked him if he even had a daughter. He confessed that he did not. I asked him "Why are you doing this?"

That's when the dam broke. He looked down and away and said he has a terrible fear of being judged. He later was diagnosed with a condition called Scopophobia, which is not a fear of being judged but a fear of being stared at. Now it all made sense. He was deathly afraid to be up in front of people and the pending presentation was sending him over the edge with having to be front and center and the focus of attention by the evaluation team on the project we were bidding on. He said all he ever wanted to do was to be a software coder, the guy behind the scenes. He was outstanding at his job, but in this particular case, the coding was a huge part of the bid and the government wanted to hear directly from the software engineers personally. He was just scared to death about it.

The next day we had a run-through and he had to do his part. He was just awful. A terrible presenter. But he was "the" guy who had to present and there wasn't much of a way around this based on the evaluator's requirements to hear from him specifically. We talked about it, and we came up with the idea of having him sit down with just his chest and face visible to the camera for the presentation. But I had him take off his shoes and put terrycloth beneath his bare feet so he could scrunch up his feet as a comfort. I also gave him a towel to put in his lap so he could wring his hands without anybody seeing him. It was painstaking and took a lot of takes and some editing, but we finally got what we needed.

After it was over, I told him I wasn't too happy about the lie he had told me. It's a serious thing and he should have just been honest with me because cutting is a very serious issue and not something to mess around with. He apologized and that was fine. It was private between us, and I knew if I had told his boss he would have been fired. But that's how debilitating these kinds of anxiety disorders can be. They can make you do things you wouldn't otherwise do.

The last story (of many, many over the years) I'll share happened in 2020. I was coaching a team for an Orals presentation and one of the team members seemed distant and very down. Again, my intuition kicked in and one evening I called him up and said, "Joe, what is bothering you? You seem to be a million miles away. Is everything okay?" There was a pause on the other end of the line, and he said, "Well, between you and me Schiffy, there is something that has shaken me up pretty badly, but I don't want the other members of the team to know."

Now part of my job requires confidentiality on a number of levels. I am often more than just a coach — I am a shoulder to cry on, a counselor of sorts and just somebody to talk to when people are hurting inside and cannot perform to their potential. I assured him anything we discuss is private and just between us. Then he broke down.

He proceeded to tell me he hadn't heard from his best friend of some 40 years in a few days. He said he got worried because it was highly unusual not to hear from him as they would talk every day. He said he had gone to his house last week as he had a spare key and had found him dead in his living room. It turns out he had been dead for three days. Needless to say, he was shocked and overwhelmed. He said in the ensuing days leading up to what he had just told me he had been dealing with his own shock and grief, and both he and his friend's family's devastation. Then he told me something which really threw me for a loop. Something I couldn't even imagine dealing with.

He looked me in the eye and said, "David, I think I can deal with the emotional loss, and it will get better over time. I know people die. But what I can't deal with is when we run through the presentation and I start talking, I cannot get the stench of the smell that hit me when I walked in to find him out of my system. I smell it on my fingers. It just happens and I can't seem to make it stop."

I didn't know what to say. I said, "Well, I can go to the management and see if we can get a replacement for you." Now this would have been a risky move as we were well into the final stages of preparing for the presentation. He wasn't having any of that. He said, "I can do this, I just need your help. Can you please help me?" I was honored and humbled at the same time and told him of course I can help you. I'll do whatever I can to get you ready."

We worked hard together to get through his problem. He ended up doing an excellent job in his role during the presentation. Sometimes these personal tragedies are kept deep inside people, and they don't want anyone to know about them. They're scared. They don't want to let the team down.

This is the secret problem facing a lot of professionals in their lives. I pass along these stories so you can get an idea of what my job is like, but more importantly in the grand scheme of things, to get a better understanding of just how awful anxiety can be and the multitude of ways it can manifest itself in a person's professional dynamics and interactions. We've come a long way in this area but have even farther to go. I strongly believe we have to break down the barriers that prevent people from seeking help and being able to overcome these often deeply personal issues.

My job is to be able to recognize that some people need extra empathy and compassion when they are called upon to walk on a stage, get in front of a camera or make any kind of presentation. They are your friends. They are your coworkers. They may be you. But when the cards are on the table, they can be helped. We can help them overcome their fears and make them better at what they do and how they do it. We can help them tap into their natural selves and find a way to help them achieve their own personal goals. That's more than a win for the team. It's a win for the human beings who comprise the team.

Remember the next time you even think about saying "just relax" to someone. You have no idea what they are dealing with inside.

EPILOGUE

"And The Beat Goes On."

And we come full circle. For now. As I mentioned at the beginning of this book, if there's anything I've done in my life it's been to *not* follow a conservative path of a career. I have let life lead me and taken the turns that have come my way. Along the way, I viewed every turn as an opportunity and I tried to seize on every one of them as best I could. I probably missed a lot of chances for a more profound career but when you think about it, it's been really quite interesting. I ended up creating a highly successful company with amazing employees, phenomenal clients and an outstanding reputation. And... I did it on my own terms. My father wanted me to be a lawyer or a doctor. You read how that turned out. Instead, I ended up falling in love with acting and the arts. I desperately wanted to be in front of an audience but ended up being behind the camera and engaging the audience through other means.

A major shift in my fortunes occurred in 1993 when my wife and I left the safety of St. Louis, where I had lived pretty much my whole life, to move to Los Angeles where I thought young men wearing plaid shirts were possibly gang members. Oh, how young and naïve I was. But if I can say one good thing about my ex-wife (we split shortly after the move to LA), she told me she wanted me to get a real job. I told her I have a real job; I'm a director and a producer. She blithely told me that wasn't a real job. She wanted me to get essentially a nine-to-five job. That push actually propelled me into marketing at Rockwell Aerospace (later merging with Boeing). Ironically, as I already had a life-long love of all things NASA, I ended up supporting the space shuttle program which got me into the world of business Orals Presentation Coaching where I eventually started what has turned out to be a very successful business working with companies seeking to win highly lucrative contracts with the Federal Government and Department of Defense.

Along the way I worked alongside Elaine Howard, then the CEO at Army Times Publishing Company. I would also be remiss without talking about both Linda Fairchild and Steve Trejo, my amazing leaders at Boeing. From Army Times I became part of an oral consultant practice with Steve Myers and Associates who had an amazing vision of life. From there I moved to Northrop Grumman, one of the world's greatest aerospace and IT companies, and met people like Don Winter, who ultimately became the secretary of the Navy. I also want to mention my ultimate mentor in life, Bob Jones, who now lives in Huntsville, Alabama. Bob was my coach in just about everything. I could listen to Bob for hours talk about his life which is very rare as I'm usually the one doing the talking. Bob told me the story about how Don Winter wanted me when I was at Boeing because I had made Northrop look bad with the trade shows I had conceived and produced for

Boeing. He wanted to get the guy who did it so he could go and make a difference in setting us up as the leader in missile defense. That was Don's vision and that's exactly what we did.

I moved on to Booz Allen Hamilton, one the world's most respected consulting firms, where I learned I absolutely did not fit in. It was the first place that told me how to dress, how to speak, and how to act — and that kind of ritualistic dynamic never worked for me. I recall we would have to fill out a six-to-eight-page form talking about ourselves; what we were doing, and what we thought our clients thought of us. It was an exhaustive and pointless exercise in my mind. At the end of it, we had to give an oral briefing of seven minutes in length in front of a C-shaped table of executives. It was adversarial to say the least.

After some examination and crunching some numbers, I realized we were spending millions of dollars in a review process which basically would reveal if an employee would get a 2.3% or a 2.6% increase in base pay. Just crazy. I remember bringing my thoughts to a senior executive who essentially told me to shut up. It was there I had a nervous breakdown and realized I will have a lifelong battle with anxiety. Around this time, I met an amazing human being named Anna Lee Hoodem who became my dearest friend and therapist — and who started me on the path to learning how to handle my anxiety, find happiness and ultimately lead me to where I am today.

I have purposely included my issues with anxiety throughout this book because I truly believe it is one of the most under-diagnosed and prevalent conditions that affects a lot more people than any of us will ever know. My anxiety produced physical, emotional and, at times, professional pain I didn't know how to deal with. But I learned — and am still learning — that you can manage the issue. This is why I so strongly encourage anyone dealing with the same issues I have to reach out if you feel you need professional help. There is no shame. Life is so very short. Like you, I'm sure, I've lost many a friend to diseases of all kinds. I have witnessed how the horrors of war can cripple the strongest among us.

I've also been around people in my life who make me laugh so hard, I think I'm going to pass out. I'm not a religious person, but I am going to use the word blessed here because I ***do*** believe I am a blessed individual who has had the benefit of having great people in my life. As my father grew into the final years of his life, I asked him what he believes will happen after he dies. "I will become worm food," was his only reply. I don't know what the future holds, however what I do know is I am thankful for all who have made my life enjoyable and worth living to the fullest.

My mother and father were very special people to me, as is my sister, who was always there for me in high school when the bullying was at its worst. She was always my best friend. I am thankful for my dear friend Louis Schwartz with whom I have done so much and still to this day is one of my closest, best friends. Like you I'm sure, there are people in my life you just lost touch with. Sometimes they pop back into your life. In fact, as I was finishing this book, I got a call from a guy who said his name was "Slurpee." I drew a big blank. He said, "Schiffy, it's Ben Thompson — Slurpee." Then the light went on. We worked very closely together at Rockwell, and I hadn't seen him since 1999. He flew in and came to my house in Delaware and from the moment we hugged, we began laughing and recalling some crazy moments from our past. It was as though time hadn't passed at all. It was great. Oh, and his nickname was given because when we were eating breakfast at Rockwell, he would get a coffee yogurt without a spoon and would slurp it down; the name was born. While at my home, Ben informed me his wife was battling terminal cancer. Ugh. Another person close to me who was going to lose somebody close to him.

Yet that is life. A dear friend of mine was the victim of sexual abuse at the hands of her father and his best friend. But she got help and is strong today with a great career and positive outlook on life. I admire her so very much.

When I reflect on all of this "stuff of life," I realize I don't have a lot to complain about. I am a lucky man. My parents survived the Holocaust. I have met some of my heroes. I get to work with the best and brightest, true contemporary great patriots in the intelligence and military communities. Most people have no idea about the risks and sacrifices these men and women have made for us to have the freedom to be keyboard commandos — and have stupid social media fights as we live free lives away from the real madness and evil which infests other parts of the world.

My journey is far from over, with movies and TV shows I'm affiliated with coming out soon and my federal consulting career hitting its peak. I have more mountains to climb and challenges to face and I am thankful I wake up safe and sound, and have those opportunities. Plus I have the new companionship of Carson (named after Johnny) to keep me company and brighten my days at the beach and in the back yard.

I also want to give a shout out to my dear friend Steve Penn who helped me write this book. Steve has always been there for me in my life and has proven to me no matter how much time passes, you never forget who your true friends are.

Finally, and most dear to my heart, is my daughter Kira, whom I adopted from China 19 years ago. Becoming a father and raising her has been the absolute greatest joy of my life. She has grown from a cute, curious little girl to a beautiful, insanely talented and intelligent young woman. She has shown me what unconditional love is truly all about. She has made me a better human being every step of the way and there are no words for me to express how deeply proud I am of her.

Kira, I love you very much. Thank you for being you. I wish you all the success and happiness you deserve in what I am sure will be a wonderful life for you.

Thank you everyone. Love to you all.

Respectfully,
Schiffy

A Surprise and horrible ending...

After completing the book around mid October of 2022, I got the most shocking call I have ever had. The very dear friend, the man who believed in me enough to help me pull together this amazing collection of stories. A person whose craft and skills allowed my voice to be heard through the eloquance of his writing...Comitted suicide.

Steve Penn was one of my dearest friends and I had the utmost of respect for him, his skill and most importantly; his friendship. Steve and I had known each other since we were in our twenties. He hired me on numerous occaisions to be his director. We would laugh together, be friends and have a lifelong love that will not soon or ever be matched.

Steve, kept the dark side of his life hidden from me. Oh how I wish he would have said anything so I could somehow help him. But people who suffer the disease of depression, sometimes get to that dark place where the only relief is to end their own life. Imagine living with such pain that the ONLY solution is to end your own life.

Steve wrote his final note starting by saying, "By the time you read this I will have left this plane of existence. I don't know what the afterlife holds or if there even is one..."

Steve, I hope wherever you are, you have found happiness. I thank you for working with me for so long to write this amazing book with me. I love you. Peace be with you my friend.

Schiffy

About The Author

David "Schiffy" Schiff is internationally recognized as the go-to Orals Coach for some of the world's largest companies and has helped them win billions of dollars by securing highly lucrative government and defense contracts. Schiffy has successfully leveraged his four Emmy Awards for directing to help people tell their stories in a profound and differentiating way. Along the way he has won hundreds of international awards for excellence in his video production work, music, and event management. Schiffy knows he is only as good as the people he surrounds himself with. Whether working with a senior defense official, a CEO, a high-level Subject Matter Expert, or an actor, Schiffy makes them better at what they do. When not off on an adventure, playing his drum kit or winning big-money contracts, Schiffy is dedicated to helping a variety of charities and foundations with his generosity and passion.